YOU CAN

Create a THINKING classroom

Sue Cowley

The best-selling author of
Getting the Buggers to Behave
and *You Can Create a
Calm Classroom*

FOR AGES
4-7

" Thinking skills are a powerful
means of improving the quality
of learning in classrooms.

DfES

Author
Sue Cowley

Editor
Sara Wiegand

Assistant Editor
Catherine Gilhooly

Illustrations
Mike Phillips

Series Designer
Catherine Mason

Designer
Lynne Joesbury

Cover concept/designer
Anna Oliwa

Cover illustration
© BananaStock/PunchStock

Text © 2006 Sue Cowley

© 2006 Scholastic Ltd

Designed using Adobe InDesign

Published by Scholastic Ltd
Villiers House
Clarendon Avenue
Leamington Spa
Warwickshire CV32 5PR

www.scholastic.co.uk

Printed by Bell and Bain Ltd.
3 4 5 6 7 8 9   7 8 9 0 1 2 3 4

British Library Cataloguing-in-Publication Data
A catalogue record for this book is available from the British Library.
ISBN 0-439-96554-3
ISBN 978-0439-96554-5

The rights of the author Sue Cowley have been asserted in accordance with the Copyright, Designs and Patents Act 1988.

Contents

Contents

Introduction

Thinking skills and learning

In recent years, there has been a surge of interest in how children think and learn and in the way that the brain works. This new focus provides a useful counterbalance to an emphasis on the content of learning. No longer is it enough to see our children as empty vessels to be filled up with facts, skills and knowledge. Instead we can see our pupils as unlit fires, just waiting for us to spark the touch paper and ignite an interest in thinking about how and why the world around them works.

Learning for life

Our aim must be to teach children more about how they learn and encourage them to use approaches and strategies for thinking that really work for them. This helps to put them on the right path to lifelong learning. Whatever subject or problem they come up against in the future, they can apply the thinking strategies necessary to help them understand and progress.

A range of thinking skills

The term 'thinking' can cover a whole range of skills, strategies and approaches. We might be teaching our children how to reason and apply logic to a problem. We could be encouraging them to take imaginative and innovative approaches to a creative endeavour. We also need to encourage them to develop the skill of metacognition. Simply put, this means teaching them to have an awareness of their own thinking processes, so that they can develop and extend these for themselves.

Making connections

A key thinking skill is the ability to make links; to see and understand the connections and patterns that exist between different ideas or subjects. Increasingly, teachers are being encouraged to return to at least some of the cross-curricular approaches that used to be so popular. This approach mirrors the way that the mind works; we develop thinking by looking for and making links, rather than by dividing our thoughts up into individual compartments.

The effective, thinking teacher

Taking an interest in developing your children's thinking should make you a better, more interesting teacher. When we look for ways of developing different thinking skills within our lessons, we are encouraged to take new and imaginative approaches to our work. Not only is this great for the children, but it also makes the whole experience of being a teacher that much more interesting and thrilling for us.

You can... Develop an effective questioning technique

How well you use questions will have a significant impact on the quality of children's thinking. However, an effective questioning technique is a surprisingly complex and tricky skill to acquire.

Thinking points

● Be aware when you ask your children lots of 'closed' questions (ones that only require a 'yes' or 'no' answer or a brief response that is either correct or incorrect).

● Think about when to use closed questions. They can help you to assess understanding and knowledge and be useful for reinforcing learning.

● When using lots of closed questions, you normally have a set answer in mind. This can stifle creative and open-ended thinking.

● 'Open' questions encourage children to think more fully, giving their thoughts, ideas and opinions. Open questions typically lead to more creative and interesting responses.

● Sessions using open questions will probably take considerably more time than those using closed ones.

Tips, ideas and activities

● Use a good mixture of closed and open questions. Where you want to generate more complex thinking about a topic, use mainly open questions.

● Use a variety of formats for question and answer sessions: as a whole class activity, individually, in pairs or groups.

● Consider why you use different types of questions and the kind of responses you hope to receive. Look at the differences between the following kinds of questions:

○ *What colour is this fire engine?*
This closed question requires a single word 'correct' answer. It tests knowledge of colours, but does not develop thinking.

○ *What else is the same colour as this fire engine?*
This open question asks for the generation of ideas, and allows children to give their own suggestions. It works well as a small group activity.

○ *This fire engine is red. It's my favourite colour because it's really bold. What is your favourite colour and why?*
This open question asks for a personal response and would be effective as an individual or paired activity.

● Work with your children to set clear rules for question and answer sessions. The photocopiable sheet 'Question and answer guidelines' (see page 56) gives you some guidelines.

● Don't always choose volunteers to answer questions; sometimes use an 'anyone can be asked to answer' approach. Give the children some thinking time first, and reserve this approach for questions where everyone can reasonably be expected to give a view, idea or opinion.

● Get your children to think about the concept of questions. Consider how:

○ Some questions don't have simple answers
○ Sometimes there is no 'right' or 'wrong' answer
○ In some curriculum areas (such as science), a key part of the subject is looking for answers to difficult questions
○ Sometimes teachers (and adults) don't know the answer to questions.

● Try responding to your children's questions with a question instead of giving an answer.

You can... Use non-verbal signals to encourage thinking

You can convey a huge amount to a class without actually opening your mouth. Your use of body language and facial expressions will often influence learning and behaviour a great deal more than what you actually say to the children.

Thinking points

● Many young children have only a limited vocabulary or understanding of spoken language. Consequently, their 'reading' of your non-verbal signals will play a key part in their responses to you and your teaching.

● Teachers will sometimes send subconscious signals through their body language and then be surprised at the way the class responds. For example, if you show a lack of confidence through defensive body language, the children might be tempted to misbehave.

● It is possible to block or discourage thinking by displaying very small facial indicators of your inner feelings and reactions, such as rolling your eyes.

● Teachers can use non-verbal signals to communicate an imaginary feeling, to better engage the class with the learning. You could look excited about a topic to enthuse the children, or confused about a question to get them thinking.

Tips, ideas and activities

● Create a break between your first, instinctive, reactions and the impressions that you give the class. For example, if a child gives what you might perceive to be a silly or weird response or idea, try not to show your feelings through your facial expressions.

● There are an enormous range of non-verbal signals that will encourage children to think. However, you will often need to make these cues a little bit larger than life so that all the children will be able to read and understand them.

● When asking a question, create a sense of involvement by looking puzzled or curious about the query you have posed. You might try:

  ● creasing up your face, particularly your forehead
  ● raising one or both eyebrows
  ● looking up towards the ceiling
  ● pursing your lips
  ● leaning back in your chair to ponder
  ● tapping your index finger on your mouth
  ● grasping your chin in your hand
  ● scratching your head
  ● sighing deeply.

● Similarly, when you want the children to generate lots of ideas about a subject, you can encourage this through some clever use of non-verbal communication. Body posture and the use of the hands are particularly important in giving a sense of urgency and interest. You could experiment with:

  ● sitting leaning forwards from the waist, elbows on knees, hands clasped together
  ● holding your hands out, palms upwards, and pulling your fingers towards yourself to indicate 'come on, give me lots of suggestions'
  ● clicking your fingers to a child who gives a good suggestion, and using short verbal comments, such as *Well done, who's next?*
  ● moving around the classroom space to give a sense of pace and energy to the pooling of ideas
  ● looking excited by good ideas, by opening your eyes and mouth wide
  ● clapping your hands in response to interesting suggestions.

You Can... Plan lessons that develop thinking skills

Thinking skills can and should be incorporated into every subject that you teach. It's about finding an approach to learning that encourages the children to think for themselves, rather than spoon-feeding them facts, information and ideas.

Thinking points

● It is tempting to assume that any lesson will be bound to get the children thinking. Unfortunately, this is not necessarily the case.

● The demands of delivering the curriculum can encourage us to deliver 'by rote' or teacher-led lessons. These lessons can stifle our pupils, rather than encourage them to think for themselves.

● There is no need for busy teachers to be constantly reinventing the wheel and planning new lessons from scratch where plans already exist. However, a lesson you have planned yourself will inevitably better suit your teaching style and your class.

● The secret is finding a balance between excessive planning and no personalised planning at all. Remember that planning new lessons can and should be a fun, inspiring and exciting part of your work.

Tips, ideas and activities

● When approaching a new topic, apply your own thinking skills to work out how it might be best delivered.
   ● Use a mind map to gather ideas (see page 16 for more information on using these).
   ● Don't narrow down your thinking too soon. Gather lots of different ideas before you decide how to deliver the topic.
   ● Don't necessarily go for the most obvious approach. Sometimes it works to take a few risks and use a really unusual idea or angle.

● We think and learn best when we are involved in actually doing something. Look for ways of turning abstract concepts into concrete, 'hands-on' activities. Use props, objects, sensory experiences, stories and so on to do this. For example, when working on the skill of sequencing during a history topic, give the children a range of interesting objects. Ask them to place these in order from oldest to newest, then discuss how they reached their conclusion.

● Use the internet, and its community of teachers, to inspire you and give you ideas. Put a message on the TES staffroom (www.tes.co.uk/staffroom) to ask other teachers how they approach a topic.

● When you plan a lesson, think carefully about the kind of questions you are going to use. Find lots of open-ended questions that will encourage the children to think for themselves. Try not to ask questions where you have a specific answer in mind. See page 6 for ways of developing an effective questioning technique.

● Where possible, involve the children in your planning. When introducing a new subject, ask the class to generate a set of questions they would like answered.

● Occasionally, deliver a lesson without a structured plan. Use an inspirational resource as a starting point and let the children decide the direction in which the learning should go.

You Can... Develop a teaching style that encourages thinking

Your approach to teaching will have a huge impact on the quality of your class's thinking. The children need to feel confident and comfortable to share their thoughts with each other and also to be inspired and enthused about the process of learning.

Thinking points

● The way that you view your role as a teacher will have an impact on the kind of style that you use with the class. Ideas about how the teacher should approach his or her work change over time.

● Teaching is very prone to fads and fashions (often from those not actually in the classroom!) about the best way to teach. There seems to be a cyclical nature to this, for example, views on topic work.

● If you truly wish to encourage thinking, sometimes you may need to disregard the pressures from above (from senior managers, education officials, the curriculum). Have the courage of your own convictions about what will work best for your children.

Tips, ideas and activities

● Consider how you see your role as a teacher and how your perceptions might limit or expand your children's thinking. Which of these approaches best describes your position?
  ● Passing on knowledge, skills and information.
  ● Delivering structured lessons.
  ● Leading the class from the front.
  ● Helping the children to learn.
  ● Working as a partner with the class.
  ● Acting as a mentor for the children.

● The format of your lessons can help encourage your children to think.
  ● Strike a balance between teacher-led, skills-based work and lessons that allow for open-ended responses.
  ● Build a sense of teamwork. Offer your children problems to solve, and work with them to find solutions.
  ● Encourage the children to use their initiative, rather than always giving them the answers.
  ● Be ready to adapt an activity or a lesson if it isn't working.
  ● Use a process of feedback, regularly asking the children for their responses.
  ● Don't talk at them too much. Aim for less teacher talk, more pupil activity!

● The way that you deliver your lessons will also have an impact on your children's thought processes.
  ● Use space in an interesting way. Don't always teach from the front.
  ● Use a varied pace. Include activities of different lengths and a range of vocal speeds.
  ● Use eye contact to show interest in what the children are saying and to check for understanding and focus.
  ● Have a well-modulated voice. Use tone to add interest.
  ● Incorporate pauses to check for focus and give time for understanding.
  ● Reinforce key points and key words, encouraging the children to search these out as well.
  ● Build confidence, never quash it. Avoid sarcasm and try never to brush away a child's ideas.
  ● Be humble. Admit that you don't always get it right or have all the answers.
  ● Have a sense of humour!

You Can... Manage group work more effectively

Group work can be a highly effective approach for developing children's thinking. However, it does need to be extremely well managed if it is going to be fully successful.

Thinking points

● Done well, group work has many benefits and should lead to more interesting and innovative thinking.

● As an approach, it encourages the sharing of ideas, opinions and information; it promotes teamwork; it helps the children learn from and think with their peers; it allows for more individual contributions to a lesson.

● Using group work might require a change of mind set from the teacher. It feels comforting to have total control of the class, when exercising whole-class teaching. 'Letting go of the reins' can feel quite daunting at first.

● Group work sometimes gets a bad reputation, being seen as a chance for the children to mess around or do nothing. When it is not well managed, this might indeed be the case. Managing group work effectively is one of the hardest teaching skills to learn.

Tips, ideas and activities

● Think carefully about the practical issues involved in managing group work. Have very clear expectations of work and behaviour and communicate these to your class.

● *How and when should the children move from whole class into groups?*
Let them go one group at a time and insist that they sit and wait in silence until the whole class is settled, before beginning the task.

● *How should I organise the groupings?*
Use a range of strategies, depending on the task: mixed ability, same ability, random groupings, group leaders and so on. Get your class used to mixing from the start and they won't think to question it.

● *How can I control overall noise levels in the room?*
Create a visual 'noise meter', for example a graph or scale on the board.

● *How can I regain the children's attention without shouting?*
Set up a non-verbal signal to indicate that you want to address the class: wave a wand, ring a bell or switch on a set of Christmas lights.

● *How can I keep the children on-task throughout the activity?*
Stop the class regularly for feedback and to check for understanding. Set specific targets to meet (five ideas, a group decision), and clear time limits (three minutes to complete this).

● *How do I manage any groups that 'finish early'?*
Have some extension tasks for those who have genuinely finished. If you suspect that the children are being lazy or sloppy, ask them to feedback their ideas to the rest of the class.

● *How do I deal with the confident child who takes over the group?*
Sometimes, allocate pre-set roles for the children to play within the group. Elect a 'leader' who is normally quiet and ask the confident child to act as 'note-taker'.

● *How can I share ideas between the groups?*
Use a 'doughnut'. Ask one volunteer in each group to raise a hand; this person then moves to the next group along and shares the ideas.

You Can... Develop your children's listening skills

Listening is a key skill in the development of thinking. It allows us to take in and process new ideas and information and it is also vital in the process of sharing our thoughts with others. Getting your children to listen, and to listen properly, is a crucial factor in developing better thinking.

Thinking points

● There is a big difference between the children hearing what the teacher says and actually listening to it! Active listening goes hand in hand with sustained concentration.

● Some children will find it much harder than others to focus on taking in ideas through listening.

● The active listener and thinker constantly searches for meaning in what he or she hears. Children can find it tiring to make sense of what they hear, especially when the teacher talks for long periods of time.

● After a while, some pupils will switch off and cease to understand what you are saying. They might appear to be listening, because they are silent. However, when questioned afterwards it becomes clear that they were not listening actively to what you said.

Tips, ideas and activities

● Help your children to understand what you say by thinking carefully about the way that you use language.

  ● Stick mainly to a simple vocabulary. Pick out some key words around each new topic and share these with the class.

  ● When you use more complicated words, give simpler ones alongside them to help all the children understand. For example, *times* and *multiplication* or *picture* and *illustration*.

  ● Use visual aids (pictures, objects, diagrams and so on) to reinforce your spoken language. This will be especially helpful for your visual learners.

  ● Use lots of repetition, rephrasing the same instruction or idea in a number of ways as part of your explanation. Don't assume that you can say something once and all the children will understand.

  ● Get lots of feedback from the class to check for understanding. When you give instructions for a task, ask for a volunteer to recount what you have said.

  ● Use a wide variety of vocal tones to help the class understand the work and feel keen to listen. Incorporate 'happy' tones (joy, excitement, enthusiasm) and also 'sad' tones (disappointment, irritation, unhappiness).

  ● Make plenty of use of non-verbal communication to back up your spoken word. Facial expressions and hand gestures are particularly helpful in putting across meaning to young children.

  ● Limit the amount of time that you talk. Try not to talk for periods of more than your children's age plus two (so, for five-year-olds, limit yourself to seven minutes of speaking time).

● Encourage active listening by throwing in a deliberate mistake from time to time. Specify a nonsense phrase that you are going to say at some point during the day, for example 'banana custard'. Give a prize to the first child to spot the mistake and raise a hand.

You Can... Help your children use metacognition

Although it sounds like a very complicated concept, metacognition simply means thinking about how we think. This is a difficult idea for young children to master, but you can help them take the first steps in thinking about their own thought processes.

Thinking points

● Much of the time we just get on with thinking, without delving into how our thinking processes actually work.

● The more aware your children are of how they think, the more able you and they will be to develop their thinking skills.

● Learning to internalise our thinking is important in effective learning. We need to encourage our children to ask themselves questions and propose possible answers in their heads.

● The better we understand our own thinking processes, the better able we are to develop our own strategies for learning.

● For example, understanding how we approach spelling helps us to master the skill (for example, mentally splitting up a word into syllables, or devising our own mnemonics to help us remember tricky words).

Tips, ideas and activities

● Encourage your children to articulate their thought processes by using questions to deepen their thinking. Train yourself to answer some questions with another question, rather than always simply providing the answer.

● Language skills play a key part in being able to verbalise thought processes. Help your class to learn the vocabulary of thinking, encouraging them to use words such as:

- think
- remember
- explain
- question
- problem
- guess
- know
- understand
- ideas
- solution.

● Paired exercises, with one child giving instructions to another, are a great way to get your children thinking about the mental steps used in completing a task. During the activity, encourage lots of talk about the thinking processes involved. Ask for one pair of children to demonstrate, or if you're brave, let the whole class do the exercise together. Here is an example to get you started.

- Explain that the task is to make a cheese sandwich.
- Discuss with the children what they need to know or do before the task begins. *What resources do they need? What should they do first? What difficulties might they encounter?*
- Provide the ingredients and add a complication. The child making the sandwich will be blindfolded and their partner has to give instructions.
- As the children undertake the activity, pause at various points to question and discuss the thinking that is taking place. Ask: *Do you have all the resources and information you need? What should you do if it starts to go wrong?*
- Once the task has been completed, encourage the children to reflect on how successful it was and the thinking that took place. Ask: *How effective was the process? Are you happy with the end result? How could you improve it? What could you do differently?*

● Experiment with these other suggestions for paired tasks.

- Build a tower with materials of different sizes and shapes.
- Guide partners around an obstacle course.
- Paint a picture.
- Complete a simple jigsaw.

You Can... Improve your children's concentration and focus

Children arrive at school with widely varying standards of concentration. Some are able to focus for long periods of time, others have very little concentration span at all. You can play an important part in helping your children develop this skill.

Thinking points

● Sustained concentration plays a key role in effective thinking and learning. We need to teach our children how to keep their focus on a task, idea or problem.

● Like any skill, concentration can be developed with time and practice.

● Children will find it easier to concentrate on some activities than on others. The varying learning styles and preferences of the pupils will affect their ability to concentrate.

● Environmental factors can help or hinder concentration. Background noise, excessive heat or cramped conditions can make it harder for us to focus.

● Much of what we class as misbehaviour is often about a lack of concentration. Low-level disruptions such as chatting, fidgeting and going off task might indicate poor concentration skills.

● Children diagnosed with attention deficit disorder (ADD) will find concentration a particularly tricky skill to master.

Tips, ideas and activities

● Look at your classroom afresh to ensure the right conditions for focused learning.

  ● *Spatial factors*
  Sit in each chair to ensure that all pupils can see the board. Space the desks so that the children don't bang into each other.

  ● *Environmental factors*
  Check your classroom is not too noisy or too hot, especially for high focus tasks such as writing.

  ● *Type of activities*
  Identify activities where your children concentrate best, for example role play or colouring. Incorporate more of these activities into your teaching.

  ● *Individual learning styles*
  Appeal to a range of learning styles, for example adding movement activities to longer periods of listening.

● There are many activities that can be incorporated into the school day to develop concentration skills. These might be used as short 'focus exercises' to settle the class or as 'breathers' to break up longer periods of learning.

  ● *Listening exercises*
  With eyes shut, ask your children to listen carefully. Start with a close focus; listening to their own breathing. Gradually widen the focus so that they listen out for noises in the room and then beyond.

  ● *Close observation*
  Give each child a simple object (a pebble, a paperclip) and ask them to look at it as though they have never seen it before.

  ● *Body part focus*
  With their eyes closed, ask the children to focus on one part of their bodies, for example a hand or foot. Tell them to feel the body part gradually becoming warmer.

  ● *Statues*
  Get the children into a comfortable position, for example lying on the floor. When you say '3, 2, 1, Freeze!' they freeze completely still, like statues, for a specific length of time. Start with about one or two minutes and gradually increase this.

You Can... Harness your children's curiosity

Young children have a natural sense of wonder about the world and about how it works. This instinctive curiosity creates a lovely sense of engagement with the learning. It goes hand in hand with the development of imaginative thinking.

Thinking points

● A key teaching skill is to find ways to make lessons and learning as engaging as possible. Where children genuinely want to find out answers and information, the learning and thinking will be authentic and long lasting. Harnessing our children's natural sense of curiosity will help us do this.

● Using children's own curiosity offers a great way of spicing up some of the more mundane activities or subjects that we might have to teach.

● The demands of the curriculum can encourage us to teach by telling and instructing, rather than by helping the children find things out for themselves.

● This 'by rote' approach to learning is at least partially to blame for the disaffection and disengagement that some older children feel about school.

Tips, ideas and activities

● Let your class map some of their learning, playing a role in determining how some lessons might proceed. When introducing a new topic, ask the children to devise questions they want answered during the course of your study.

● Inspire your children's sense of curiosity by working with hidden objects. When we can't see something, this makes us want to know what it is even more! You might 'hide' objects:
  ○ in a cardboard box or a treasure chest
  ○ in a sealed envelope
  ○ under a carpet or sheet
  ○ in an interesting-looking bag
  ○ outside, in the playground or nature area.

● Use a fictional scenario to add even more interest to 'hidden objects' activities.
  ○ Show the class a box which is taped up tight and has big red warning labels all over it.
  ○ Hold the box in a way that inspires curiosity, for example making it shake or look very heavy.
  ○ Talk with the children about what you should do. Ask: *Is it wise to open the box or not? What do you think might be inside?*

● Use 'I wonder' questions to spark your children's sense of curiosity. As you ask the questions, aim to look and sound puzzled yourself, to draw the class in.
  ○ I wonder what this is?
  ○ I wonder what this does?
  ○ I wonder what will happen if...?
  ○ I wonder what has happened?
  ○ I wonder how this works?

● Devise fictional scenarios to inspire lots of these 'I wonder' questions.
  ○ Put a set of muddy footprints across the classroom and open a window wide.
  ○ Remove one, fairly obvious, item from the room. For example, a favourite toy or your story-time chair.
  ○ Leave a few clues, such as a ransom note or a secret map.
  ○ When the children come in, pretend you are busy and that you haven't noticed the mess.
  ○ Ask the class to solve the mystery of where the object has gone.

You Can... Encourage your children to think about their behaviour

All teachers want their children to behave themselves. That way we can get on with the job of actually teaching them. To ensure real and long-term changes, we need the children to take a conscious, thinking part in managing their own behaviour.

Thinking points

● Empathy is a key skill in thinking about behaviour and understanding how our own behaviour can make others feel.

● Where children can be shown how their misbehaviour impacts on others, this can help them to see why change is needed.

● A very good test of whether classroom or school rules will work is whether they are fair and reasonable.

● If expectations of behaviour are reasonable, teachers are put in a strong position. There is no need to negotiate, because everyone concerned sees the rules as 'fair'.

● Where teachers are asked to apply unreasonable standards, it is inevitable that at least some children will refuse to comply. This can cause unnecessary tensions and confrontations.

Tips, ideas and activities

● Encourage your children to take ownership of their class rules.
  ● At the start of the year, set your rules in conjunction with the class.
  ● Ask the children what rules they need and why they need them.
  ● Get them to make class rules posters and display these around the room.
  ● When pupils break a rule, remind them of the thinking behind it.
  ● Use regular feedback and revision. If a rule is regularly broken, ask the class why this is and whether the rule needs adapting.

● Talk to your children about suitable punishments for different types of misbehaviour, both at school and in the world outside. You may find that they are more militant about sanctions than you!

● Drama helps build understanding and empathy. The photocopiable sheet 'Thinking about behaviour' (see page 57) gives you some scenarios to use. Use the pictures to explore and think about behaviour with your class.
  ● Talk about what is going on in the pictures.
  ● Discuss who is in the right and who is in the wrong in each situation.
  ● Ask the pupils to re-enact the scenarios, taking on a different role each time.
  ● Get feedback from the children about how it feels to be each of the characters.

● Use 'the choice' to manage misbehaviour. Here is how it works:
  ● The child misbehaves, for example, scribbling on a neighbour's work.
  ● Offer a choice, stating the right behaviour and outlining the consequences of continued wrong behaviour.
  ● For example, *I want you to stop scribbling on Neisha's work now and say sorry. If you carry on scribbling, I will move you to sit somewhere else.*
  ● Step away for a moment to let the child make the right decision.
  ● If the child continues to misbehave, calmly apply the sanction you have outlined.

You Can... Teach structures for thinking

Learning how to organise and structure their thinking is a key skill for your children to learn. At this age their written vocabulary may be fairly limited. However, there are still lots of effective ways in which they can record and structure their thoughts.

Thinking points

- When you first approach a topic, gather lots of information and ideas. Find out what your children already know or think about the subject.

- 'Spidergrams' or 'scattergrams' offer the ideal format for this kind of thinking, because they capture initial thoughts in one place. You can then help your class to arrange, sort and develop their thinking.

- Our natural impulse is to organise our thinking, typically by creating patterns and web-like structures that help us find connections and links between different ideas.

- Considering where things go in relation to one another is a vital part of developing thinking. 'Mind maps' offer a very useful way of linking ideas.

- The structures we create normally have one central thought, which then branches out into smaller or more detailed ideas, gradually moving further from the initial stimulus.

Tips, ideas and activities

- Spidergrams are a vital structure for thinking. Consider ways of using them to the maximum effect.
  - When creating whole-class spidergrams, ask the children where you should put each idea and why.
  - Look at how distance can indicate how closely linked two ideas are. For example, close together = clear link, distant = less obvious connection.
  - Don't edit out unusual or apparently irrelevant ideas. Often, these are examples of really interesting, lateral thinking.
  - When a child brings up a seemingly unrelated idea, talk with the class about where you might 'store' it temporarily (perhaps in a small box right at the edge of your diagram).
  - Use colour, symbols and images to enhance your diagrams. Ask your children to consider the most appropriate colours or pictures to use.
  - Experiment with multimedia spidergrams. Hand out magazines and ask the children to make collage diagrams around a topic.
  - On a dry day, take the class outside to do a huge spidergram in chalk on the playground floor.

- Mind maps are a development of the classic spidergram. A single image or idea is placed in the centre and this is mapped outwards to connected thoughts by the use of lines or other symbols. Try developing some of your class diagrams into more complex mind maps. For more information, refer to *Mind Maps for Kids* by Tony Buzan (HarperCollins).

- Discuss the range of symbols you might use to link ideas and enhance thinking. The sheet 'Symbols for thinking' (see page 58) provides lots of examples. Use it with your class to:
  - Identify each symbol and with older children, write the symbol names on the sheet
  - Talk and think about what the various symbols mean
  - Discuss where the children might have seen or used these symbols before
  - Consider how they might be used within a spidergram or mind map
  - Provide 'cut-outs' for some spidergrams or mind maps.

You Can... **Explore ways of improving memory**

Knowing how to use your memory well is important for academic success and also in the world beyond the school gates. Being able to remember things will help your children learn spellings, memorise facts and information, and do well in their tests and future exams.

Thinking points

● Some people feel that they have a 'bad memory' and are not very good at remembering things. But memory is a skill just like any other. With work and the right strategies it can be developed and improved.

● We tend to remember much better when something is particularly vivid to us. These 'vivid' people, places or situations might stick in our minds for countless years after the event itself.

● Memories can be made 'vivid' in a variety of ways. Often, negative encounters will stick with us far longer than more pleasant ones. Any event that is very unusual or special, such as a birthday party or a trip somewhere new, will also tend to stick in the mind.

● Smells and scents can be a very powerful trigger to memory, with the briefest whiff of a food being enough to pull you back into the past.

Tips, ideas and activities

● Play 'Kim's Game'.
  ● Put about ten small objects on a tray, and cover them.
  ● Show the objects to the class for one minute.
  ● Cover the objects again and ask the children to list as many as they can.
  ● To make the game harder, add a time gap between showing and listing the objects.
  ● Some children will find this game easy. Talk about the kind of thinking that they are doing to help themselves remember.

● Teach your class some memory strategies, replaying 'Kim's Game' afterwards to see how well they work. Memory techniques work by forming connections and links, creating a chain of thought so that one item sparks off the memory of another.
  ● *Story linking*
  Get your children to create a story that ties all the items together, the weirder and more vivid the better! For example, if three of the items are a ball, a stick and a one pound coin, you might create a story in which a boy throws a ball for his dog and the dog suddenly disappears. He finds the dog fighting over a huge stick with a crocodile. He throws the coin at the crocodile, hitting him on the nose so that he lets go.
  ● *Number memory rhymes*
  Choose a rhyming word for numbers one to ten, for example 'one – sun', 'two – shoe' and so on. Link each of the ten objects to one of the numbers. For example, for one, imagine the ball up in the sky, looking like the sun. For two, visualise the stick inside a shoe, so that walking feels really uncomfortable.
  ● *Sensory impressions*
  Encourage the class to come up with powerful sensory responses to each of the objects. For instance, if the ball is red, imagine holding it and feeling that is very hot, burning your hands. Similarly, the pound coin might feel very cold and heavy.

You Can... **Look for links, patterns and connections**

It is an instinctive part of human nature to search for links, patterns and connections. In fact, this mirrors the way that we think. Neurons connect to each other inside our brains, with our thoughts passed from cell to cell as electrical impulses.

Thinking points

● The first step in finding links between things is to understand how to sort and classify them.

● Once children can identify how and why some things are similar and others are different, they can look for the connections and patterns between them.

● Sorting and linking activities offers lots of opportunities for hands-on, physical involvement by the children.

● The more actively involved the children are in the tasks, the more likely they are to understand and remember.

● Young children can find it hard to sort by more than one criteria (eg, that something can be both the same size and the same shape). This is a skill that needs to be developed during the first years at school.

Tips, ideas and activities

● Encourage the children to explore different ways of sorting. This exercise requires good self-discipline from the children. It also requires them to cooperate and work as a team. Depending on your class, you may need to build up in stages to the whole-class activity.

  ● Ask for about five to ten volunteers to stand in front of the class.
  ● Invite the children to suggest some things that are similar and different about the volunteers, for example, hair colour, gender, age.
  ● Now sort your volunteers in a range of ways as suggested by the class, grouping those that are the same together.
  ● Once the children have the idea, take the whole class into a large space, for example, the playground or hall.
  ● Ask everyone to freeze, in total silence, in a space.
  ● Call out a sorting criterion, such as 'Same eye colour'.
  ● Use a stopwatch and challenge the class to see how quickly they can sort themselves.
  ● If the children need additional help, identify the different sets with the class before they sort themselves. You might also specify where each set should go (for example, 'Cat owners here', 'Dog owners here').
  ● Try these other suggestions for sorting criteria, ranging from the simple to the very tricky! Girl/boy; hair length; brothers/sisters/no siblings; type of pets; month of birth. With older classes, try sorting by two criteria at once, for example, length and colour of hair.

● Look at patterns in the natural world. Collect different materials such as leaves, seeds, seed pods, sticks and stones.

● Do some 'Odd one out' exercises, looking for patterns of similarity. In some instances, there may be more than one logical 'odd one out' and this can lead to some interesting thinking and discussion work. Ask the class to find the odd one out in the following lists:

  ● sea, river, pond, tap
  ● horse, cow, cat, dog
  ● door, window, gate, mirror.

You Can... Encourage creative and lateral thinking

Some thinking helps us make sense of the world, for instance through the use of logic and the search for patterns of meaning. Creative and lateral thought allows us to generate and develop new and innovative ideas.

Thinking points

● A key feature of our brains is the recognition of familiar patterns. Although not all cars look the same, we can see that they fall into the generic 'car' category.

● Much of the time, our thinking follows linear paths and routes. One idea leads to another and then another.

● Lateral thinking asks us to break away from pattern recognition and linear thought, to look for random ideas and novel solutions.

● Lateral thought tends to feel like an intuitive rather than a logical response to a question. It is about random inspiration, the classic 'light bulb' moment, rather than step-by-step critical thinking.

● Many terms and phrases have been used to describe this type of thought: 'thinking outside the box', ideas 'from out of left field', 'blue skies thinking'.

Tips, ideas and activities

● Use a fictional problem-solving exercise to help your children understand more about creative and lateral thought.

  ● Choose a fairy tale, for example 'The Three Little Pigs'.
  ● Re-read the tale and talk through the story together.
  ● Ask the class to identify the central problem faced by the characters. In this instance, *How can I build a house so that the wolf can't get in?*
  ● Divide the class into groups and ask each group to come up with at least five solutions to the problem. At first, they may take a very linear approach, for example build a metal house, with bars on the windows and a strong door.
  ● Gather the class together and ask each group to feedback some of their best ideas. Identify any examples of creative or lateral thinking.
  ● Add an additional problem, forcing them to think laterally: *The wolf develops super powers. No matter how strong you build the house, he can still blow it down.*
  ● Discuss how and why the initial problem has now changed.
  ● In groups look for more solutions. Encourage the children to think laterally, using the techniques given below.

● Here are some ways of facilitating creative thinking.

  ● Look at the question from the opposite side or angle. For example, *Make friends with the wolf instead!*
  ● Move away from logic to come up with 'crazy' or 'silly' ideas and then consider how you might make them work. For example, *Create a hologram of a house to fool the wolf.*
  ● Rephrase the question so that you come at it from a different angle. For example, *How can I keep myself safe from the wolf? By living in a tent and creating an early warning system so that I can run away before he arrives.*
  ● Switch the perspective to look at the issue from the angle of another character. For example, *Build a prison for the wolf rather than a house for the pigs.*

You Can... Use story time to develop thinking

Stories offer a wealth of opportunities for the development of thinking. They are great for developing imaginative thought, empathy and engagement. They can also provide a way into thinking skills such as problem solving, evaluation and reflection.

Thinking points

● Listening to a story will help your children develop their listening skills and also to increase concentration spans.

● Stories help us to develop empathy and understanding, as we see how other people or characters might experience emotions, solve problems and face up to situations.

● Stories allow us to experience scenarios and meet people beyond the realm of our direct experience. For those children whose experiences of the world are limited, stories will play a particularly important role.

● Young children absolutely love to listen to stories. There is something very magical about seeing your class engrossed as you tell them a story.

Tips, ideas and activities

● Before you read a new story to the class:
  ● Show the cover of the book and ask them to talk about what they think might happen.
  ● Tell the class the title of the story and ask them to predict possible characters or events.
  ● Ask the children to think about and list some words that might be in the story. Refer back to this list after you have read the story.

● As you read a story:
  ● Ask the children to close their eyes, to block out any distracting input from their other senses.
  ● Invite the class to add sound effects, or to join in with any repetition.
  ● Pause half way through, and ask the children to say what is happening in their minds as they listen.
  ● Talk about how we can 'picture' a story in our heads, noting the way that different people will 'see' different versions of the same people and events.

● After reading a story:
  ● Ask the children to represent the events of the story or their feelings about it in a picture.
  ● Use a quick-fire question and answer session to test for understanding.
  ● Pick out the key events and put them in sequence.
  ● Use a storyboard to order the most important events.
  ● Talk about the feelings and motivations of the main characters.
  ● Help your children pick out any interesting use of language, for example repetition or alliteration.
  ● Ask the pupils to recall five key words from the story.
  ● Arrange the children into pairs to retell the story to a partner.
  ● Arrange the children into groups to prepare a 'freeze-frame' of one event in the story. Ask the class to guess which moment is being shown.
  ● Identify parts of the story where a character has to solve a problem. Talk about how the problem gets solved, and whether there are any other ways to resolve it.

You Can... Use the senses to stimulate thinking

We might consider thinking to be very much a cerebral activity, unconnected to what goes on in our bodies. In fact, sensory responses can spark a great deal of creative thought. They can also help young children understand more about their world.

Thinking points

● For many of us, sight is the sense through which we engage most fully with the environment around us.

● In the classroom, we also expect our children to use their hearing a great deal, whilst we tend to give less weight to the senses of touch, taste and smell.

● Removing one sense can help us respond more strongly with our other senses, for example, asking your children to smell different foods with their eyes shut.

● Taking away a sense on which the children rely heavily, such as sight or hearing, can help with the development of empathy.

● Using a blindfold or ear plugs can help both children and teachers understand how it feels to be visually- or hearing-impaired.

Tips, ideas and activities

● Set up a 'tactile tunnel' or a 'tactile tent' in your classroom. Creating a dark, enclosed area will help the pupils respond with senses other than their sight.

   ● To maintain concentration and the right atmosphere, send in only limited numbers of pupils at a time.

   ● Consider how you want your children to respond after spending time in the tent or tunnel. You might specify this yourself, or leave it as an open-ended decision for each child.

   ● There are many possible response options: discussions, drawing, modelling, creative writing, poetry, music-making, movement activities and so on.

   ● Involve the class in deciding what should go in the space, or you could devise it yourself as a surprise for them.

   ● Try using a range of sensory stimuli, providing different experiences over the course of a few days or weeks (see below).

● For a touch experience, you could include:

   ● Materials to handle: clay, foil, plastic, bubble wrap, metal, different papers, stones.

   ● Textures to feel: silk, velvet, cork, scouring pads, feathers.

   ● If you're brave, a 'mucky-yucky' version: jelly, glue, paint, wallpaper paste, porridge.

● For a taste experience, you could include:

   ● Fruit and vegetables: lemons, grapes, carrots, lettuce.

   ● Foods from around the world: curry, pasta, croissants.

   ● Different liquids: milk, water, fruit juices, cold tea.

● For a smell experience, you could include:

   ● Pleasant smells: jasmine, hyacinth, rose petals, lemon, menthol, herbs, spices such as cumin and coriander.

   ● Unpleasant smells: wet wool, sour milk, boiled eggs.

● For a sound experience, you could include:

   ● Instrumental sounds: bells, drums, whistles, maracas.

   ● Objects and materials: paper rustling, metal clinking, plastic crunching.

   ● Clips of classical, world or pop music.

   ● Extracts from a sound-effects tape.

You Can... Use displays to develop thinking

A bright, interesting and stimulating classroom environment can really help us to engage our children and get them actively participating in lessons. Displays can play a key role in creating this sense of a vibrant and positive environment.

Thinking points

● There can be a tendency to view displays as a static 'snapshot' of work that the children have previously produced.

● Where you want your classroom displays to encourage and develop thinking skills, try to view them more as a 'work in progress'.

● 'Thinking' displays will relate directly to the learning that is currently going on in your classroom. This might be as an inspiration for the work, as a part of the lessons, or as a reminder of thinking that has already taken place.

● Where support staff or classroom assistants take on responsibility for producing displays, explain how these new approaches work.

● Having a piece of work displayed will also act as a reward, motivating your children by 'showing off' what they have done to a wider audience.

Tips, ideas and activities

● Use visual thinking structures, such as spidergrams and mind maps, in your displays (see page 16). Encourage the children to see a display as something to which they can add to, rather than as a static 'end result'.

● Get your children to interact with their classroom displays.

  ● Pose questions within a display and give the children some lesson time in which to add their answers.

  ● Have a pad of sticky notes beside a display and encourage your pupils to post up their thoughts and ideas.

  ● Put lift-up flaps on a display, to encourage the children to look more closely.

  ● Use Velcro to stick up pictures, so that they can be moved around.

  ● Have a 'thinking box' as part of a display, so that children can post their thoughts and ideas about a topic. Share these thoughts, perhaps once a week

● Think carefully about the spatial aspects of the display work in your room.

  ● Check that displays are at the children's level and not at your own.

  ● Sometimes, put displays at below eye level, to encourage the children to take a fresh perspective.

  ● Add vertical interest by using banners and hanging displays. In a room with high ceilings, this can also help to lower the sense of ceiling height.

● Think in three dimensions when you create displays. For example, you could put a table in front of a display, with some objects on it relating to the topic. Set aside time during the lesson for children to explore and talk about these objects. You could also use packaging, such as cereal boxes or egg boxes, to give an added dimension to wall-mounted displays.

● Make sure that your display work reflects a range of cultural backgrounds, particularly those of the pupils in your class. Include a range of languages on your walls and encourage the children to hunt out examples of words that they recognise.

You Can... Appeal to a range of learning styles

As teachers we instinctively know that different children prefer to learn in different ways. Some pupils can listen really well, some respond enthusiastically to visual activities, whilst others are far more keen on active, movement-based tasks.

Thinking points

● The idea that children have different preferred 'styles' of learning has become increasingly fashionable and popular.

● There is currently some debate about the scientific basis for 'learning styles' theories.

● With large numbers of children in a class, it is unrealistic to expect teachers to differentiate each task for visual, auditory or kinaesthetic learners.

● However, the children will certainly benefit where the teacher uses a variety of teaching approaches in his or her lessons. This outcome is perhaps the main advantage of the current focus on 'learning styles' theories.

Tips, ideas and activities

● When planning, include a range of approaches, so that the children are seeing, hearing and doing during each lesson. When teaching from previously written schemes of work, check that these include different learning styles.

● Suggestions for auditory learning:
  ○ Use a short extract of music as the children enter in the morning, or as they come in after break
  ○ Gradually fade the music, challenging the children to be sitting ready to learn the moment it stops
  ○ Match the music to the lesson you are going to teach. Talk with the children about the mood or feelings it has created and how that might relate to the learning
  ○ Use lots of short vocal activities: chanting word or letter sounds, singing nursery rhymes, saying tongue twisters
  ○ Use a wide range of tones in your voice and, if you can, incorporate different accents or funny voices.

● Suggestions for visual approaches:
  ○ Incorporate pictures, symbols, photographs and short video clips into lessons
  ○ Use flash cards, encouraging the children to make image cards for different subjects
  ○ Show the class a flash card with the image partly covered up and gradually reveal the picture. Ask the children to identify the image as soon as possible, talking afterwards about how they did this
  ○ Use coloured cards to get your children talking about their moods and emotions.

● Suggestions for activities involving movement and practical approaches to learning:
  ○ Break up your lessons with some short exercises. For example, ask the children to draw some 'lazy 8s' in the air (the number 8 on its side)
  ○ Whenever you do work involving verbs, make a point of getting the children to actually 'do' the actions
  ○ Involve the children as volunteers and in physical demonstrations; in counting activities or making letter shapes with their bodies
  ○ Find interesting and imaginative ways for your children to move around the room; for example, move as though there is glue on the floor or in zero gravity.

You Can... Develop a thinking role play area

Your role-play area, or home corner, offers you some wonderful opportunities for developing thinking skills. The thinking your children do will be of a wide range of types, including imaginative, creative, problem solving and logical.

Thinking points

● Being involved in role play and drama helps your children think about the experience of being someone or something else.

● This understanding of how other people think and feel is central to the development of empathy.

● A role-play area also helps develop skills such as sharing, team work and cooperative play.

● Playing in a 'home corner' can be particularly helpful for those children from a background where social skills have not been well developed.

● We might tend to think of drama as being about a 'performance' shown to the class. In fact, some of the best learning will take place where the children 'become' characters in an unplanned and unscripted improvisation.

Tips, ideas and activities

● Don't feel that you must always set up and specify the 'location' of your role-play area. Involve the children in the decision-making process. Give them a range of materials and let them decide what the role-play area is and how it should be set up. Use non-specific resources: benches, bed sheets, blank paper, pegs, empty packaging.

● In a teacher-devised role-play area, you can develop more complex thinking skills by introducing some 'problems' for the children to solve.

  ○ In a shop, one of the characters loses his/her purse.
  ○ In an office, someone spills ink on an important report.
  ○ In a hospital, a patient is brought in covered with huge red spots.
  ○ In a post office, a customer brings in a package which is making strange noises.

● Use a story about a 'magic carpet' to inspire and role play some imaginative journeys.

  ○ Talk through the photocopiable sheet 'The magic carpet' (see page 59) with your class.
  ○ Discuss what is happening in each picture and where the children might be about to go in the last one.
  ○ Find a magical-looking Persian-style carpet, big enough for small groups of children to sit on.
  ○ Split the class into groups to devise an improvisation based on the pictures and to decide what happens next.
    ○ Either ask each group to perform their story to the class, or set up a 'magic carpet' corner where the children can role play different stories.

● Leave some 'puzzle objects' in your role-play area for the children to explore and discuss. Encourage them to hypothesise about what these objects are, what they are doing here and what should be done with them. For example:
  ○ In a railway station, a battered suitcase or an old-fashioned looking teddy
  ○ In a supermarket, a handbag that someone has left behind by mistake
  ○ In a toy shop, a box with a big red warning sign, 'do not open'.

You Can... Turn your classroom into 'somewhere else'

As an environment for learning, schools can be rather uninspiring places. A class trip to 'somewhere else' can really enhance the children's learning. Take this concept one step further, by creating that 'somewhere else' (whether real or imaginary) in your classroom. Use these ideas as starting points.

Thinking points

- Turning your entire classroom space into 'somewhere else' creates a magical atmosphere in which your children can learn.

- You can base work on a whole range of subjects around a single location.

- Ensure that the children participate in preparing and setting up the location. The research and preparation involved will offer many learning and thinking opportunities.

- Combine this idea with a school trip, either as a precursor to the visit, or as a way of reinforcing and extending the learning afterwards.

- Work with some visiting artists, writers or musicians to add further depth and interest. If other teachers are keen, this could develop into a whole-school project, perhaps once a term.

- Invite parents into school to visit your 'somewhere else' classroom, to see what the children have achieved.

Tips, ideas and activities

- The rainforest
  - Huge tree collages on the walls, three-dimensional birds and animals hanging from the ceiling.
  - Sound-effects tapes with animal sounds. These could be made by the children using voices and instruments.
  - Samples and pictures of foods and other resources that come from the rainforest.
  - A 'water feature' to show how the heat causes condensation.
  - Films of rainforest animals.
- The woods
  - Big tree pictures on the walls, a carpet of dried leaves (real or made) on the floor.
  - Samples of different woodland plants and bulbs to investigate.
  - Sound tapes of different native bird songs.
  - Range of woodland 'foods' for different animals: seeds, nuts, worms and so on.
  - Story books that feature woods, for example 'Little Red Riding Hood' and 'Hansel and Gretel'.
- The beach
  - Big sea collage on the walls.
  - Sand-play area with buckets, spades, diggers and so on.
  - Large tanks with water and different resources to look at floating and sinking, and also at ways of making waves.
  - Safety in the sun equipment to explore: hats, clothing, umbrellas and sun creams.
  - Rubber rings, armbands, even boats, dinghies and surfboards if you can get hold of them!
  - Poems and stories based on the sea.
  - Artistic interpretations of the sea through the ages.
- The 'land of lights'
  - Windows darkened with black paper or blackout material.
  - Christmas lights stringed around the walls and ceilings.
  - Different light sources: torches, lanterns, lamps and so on.
  - Materials for creating shadows: sheets and silhouette shapes, a tent with a light source inside.
  - A range of mirrors and other reflective surfaces, such as foil.
  - Peephole cameras, telescopes, binoculars, kaleidoscopes.

You Can... **Present thinking assemblies**

Assemblies offer a great opportunity for the pupils to gather together and celebrate all the positive things that are happening in their school. By using assembly time to highlight thinking skills, you can boost the profile of thinking across the school.

Thinking points

● The traditional assembly format leaves little room for thinking to take place, because it tends to be a 'show and tell' event. A teacher shows something of interest to the audience and tells them about it.

● It is harder to manage an assembly that encourages thinking, because you will want the children to talk about or respond to what you say.

● Whenever possible, involve the children in preparing and presenting assemblies. This will keep them engaged and encourage them to use a range of thinking skills.

● Assemblies are often viewed as 'one-off' events that do not require any particular follow-up. Challenge this idea by setting tasks or activities for the children (and their teachers) arising out of what takes place in assembly time.

Tips, ideas and activities

● Set up a rota to ensure that each class prepares and presents an assembly, perhaps once each term. Encourage teachers to hand the reins over to their children. Make the emphasis less on a 'polished performance' and more on developing ideas and sharing thinking.

● Assembly time is often used to celebrate academic, sporting or other successes. Consider how you might also use it to highlight success in thinking. You could create some new award certificates for thinking skills.

● Use lots of performance-based approaches to engage with your audience and grab their interest. One of the most engaging assemblies I've ever seen was on road safety. It started with the deputy head cycling into the hall on his bike! Consider how you might use:

  ● Lighting; for example stage lights, candles, torches, fairy lights

  ● Props and costumes; shy children could 'model' a costume or hold a prop, rather than making a verbal contribution

  ● Music; this can be great for setting the tone and can also help you create a mood and time for reflection

  ● Active audience participation and involvement; get volunteers up on stage to take part.

● Invite parents to contribute to a special assembly and use this time to challenge typical thinking about gender roles. For example:

  ● Hold a 'Mums' Assembly' where mums talk about what they do outside of the traditional home-making roles. If possible, involve any mums who work in a profession normally associated with men, such as plumbing or engineering.

  ● Hold a 'Dads' Assembly', again to challenge gender stereotypes and to encourage boys to think more widely. For example, dads could come in and talk about the range of ways in which they use reading at work or at home. This could form part of a drive to improve standards of boys' writing in your school.

You Can... **Encourage thinking among your staff**

Where the staff feel ownership of what goes on in their school, this helps immensely in keeping them well motivated. Asking all staff to think about, and participate in, the day-to-day running of the school will have a very positive overall impact.

Thinking points

● Tradition and continuity play a valuable part in the success and effectiveness of a school. However, we can also get trapped into patterns of thinking and ways of doing things that become stale and uninteresting.

● In teaching, new ideas about learning are constantly being developed, tried and tested. Keeping up-to-date with the latest approaches is not only important, it can be fun as well.

● It's vital to really think about any new educational ideas and how they might be useful (or not) for your children and your particular school situation.

Tips, ideas and activities

● People can be nervous about sharing their ideas, particularly in a small school. To overcome any reticence:
   ○ Create an 'ideas box' in which staff can post suggestions anonymously
   ○ Open the box on a weekly basis to read the ideas
   ○ Discuss the ideas in a staff meeting
   ○ Change the 'theme' of the box each week: 'creating links with parents', 'the school show' and so on.

● Encourage all staff to think about the running of the school. Often someone other than a teacher will best understand a particular area of the school. For example, canteen staff will have plenty of ideas about how lunches can be improved.

● Create a 'thinking board' in the staff room, and ask staff to post up good ideas or tips, so that these can be shared across the school. This might include:
   ○ Invitations to visit a classroom, to see some great work that the children have done
   ○ A really effective way of handling a common behaviour issue. This is especially helpful for non-teaching staff
   ○ Details of good resources and where to access them
   ○ Ideas for unusual or successful rewards
   ○ Positive notes about children's work or behaviour, so that staff can back this up with compliments outside of the classroom.

● Teachers can become isolated in their own classroom spaces. The best thinking takes place when people can bounce ideas off each other, so find ways to share good practice.
   ○ Try team teaching; joining classes so that two teachers and two assistants work together
   ○ Watch other teachers at work; this is particularly useful for new staff
   ○ Ask children to do some lesson observations and give constructive feedback to their teachers
   ○ Have a 'sharing day' when children and teachers go into each other's classes to show examples of their work.

● Think 'outside the box' about timetabling and deployment of staff. You might organise a class swap for part or all of a day, to make the best use of subject specialisms.

You Can... Create a thinking playground

Children learn a great deal through outdoor exploration and play. Although facilities for play time vary widely from school to school, there will be opportunities for developing thinking skills no matter how limited your outside space.

Thinking points

● The playground is a great place for the children to watch and learn from each other. Your younger pupils will aspire to what the older children do, so remind them to set a good example.

● We might think of the playground as a place for the children to let off steam. But play time is not just about physical fitness; it is also about creative play, learning more about the world and so on.

● The playground is also a great space for some of the messier lesson time activities, such as sand and water play and painting.

● Because of the open nature of the space, there need to be very clear boundaries and rules for playground behaviour.

● It is very important that playground supervisors are given good training in managing behaviour and effective support in applying any playground rules that are set.

Tips, ideas and activities

● Use the playground in lesson time, as well for breaks.
  ● Head out into the sunshine for a 'philosophical' discussion.
  ● Send the children out to gather information, for example taking measurements.
  ● Create role-play areas outside, such as a 'beach' or 'magic forest'.

● Get your children to redesign the playground area; this gives lots of opportunities for developing thinking across the curriculum. First, conduct an audit of current provision. Think about:
  ● How to research and gather relevant information.
  ● How to work out which equipment is used most and which least.
  ● Devising a list of questions to interview other pupils.
  ● How to record and use the information gathered.
  ● How to find and evaluate some really imaginative ideas.

● Get the children thinking 'outside the box' for their playground design. Think about:
  ● Dimensions; consider what goes up (climbing equipment), on the ground (hopscotch) and even consider changing the shape of the landscape.
  ● Different ways to use the space; for play but also for quiet reflection.
  ● Cross-curricular uses for the playground; for example, painting grids on the floor to use in maths.
  ● How the playground might be used at different times of the year and outside of play time; for example for artistic 'events' such as a concert.
  ● Who else might need to 'share' the space; animals in a nature area as well as other people.
  ● Unusual uses for playground space; for example, growing vegetables or keeping livestock.

● Ask the children to devise ground rules for play time. They could:
  ● Create a poster of rules for using equipment; its safe usage, how it will be stored and repaired and so on.
  ● Take digital photos to show children following the rules; for example, playing well with each other, taking turns.
  ● Try using peer mediators rather than staff to settle disputes.

You Can... **Think about healthy eating**

We cannot force our children to eat healthily, but what we can do is get them thinking about their food. Understanding where food comes from and how it is grown and prepared, will help your children make considered choices about what they eat.

Thinking points

● Intuitively, many teachers will see a link between children eating well and drinking plenty of water, and better behaviour and concentration.

● Children who are used to unhealthy food at home might find it hard to make sudden changes to their diet. Accept that the process could take some time.

● With the increase in packaged and processed food, we have lost the link between digging something up out of the soil, washing, cooking and then eating it. Rediscovering this link is not only important for promoting healthy eating, it is also great fun for the children.

Tips, ideas and activities

● Think about growing some food with your children. The hands-on experience of raising crops is great for getting children interested in what they eat. It also offers lots of scope for learning, particularly in science. You could:
  ● Dig up part of a grassed area to build some raised beds.
  ● Grow vegetables in pots; these can be made from recycled materials such as bins, empty cans or old tyres.
  ● Approach your local garden centre to donate compost and seeds.
  ● Involve each year group in growing one crop from seed, perhaps as a cross-years competition.
  ● Create a compost heap and teach the children about decomposition.
  ● If this all sounds a bit daunting, start by growing potatoes; they are almost impossible to get wrong.

● Introduce your children to a range of fruits, perhaps linked to work on the senses.
  ● Get the children to feel and smell different fruits with their eyes shut.
  ● Find words to describe them: kiwi/furry; pineapple/prickly and so on.
  ● Think about shells and skins: *Why do fruits have them? Why do we need to remove them?*
  ● Explore different ways of peeling fruits.
  ● Think of ideas for getting into a coconut shell.

● Set up some displays in and around your dining hall, to get the children thinking about unusual foods. You could have:
  ● A food 'Theme of the week', focusing on foods from different countries.
  ● A 'Guess the vegetable' competition, with unusual and exotic vegetables to taste and name.
  ● A 'Pin the fruit on the world' competition, with the children guessing the countries of origin.

● Encourage your children to think about how far their food has travelled.
  ● Invite local farmers in to talk to the class about their produce.
  ● Take your class on a trip to a local farm.
  ● Visit a supermarket depot to see how food is transported.
  ● Show the class how many air miles go into a take away pizza. Look at the following internet page, www.assemblies.org.uk/standing/s_pizza.html.

You Can... **Build thinking links across the school**

Creating a sense of community within a school will have a powerful impact on thinking, learning and behaviour. The children feel a sense of responsibility for their school 'family' and this helps foster a sense of mutual respect.

Thinking points

● Thinking needs to be seen as something that happens throughout the school, rather than in the classrooms of some teachers.

● All staff need to take similar approaches in order to change the learning culture to one where *how* we learn is as important as *what* we learn.

● Where the children are closely involved in the running and development of the school, this helps them feel more ownership of their learning.

● Where the children feel that they are in control of their own education, this leads to improved attitudes, behaviour and application to the work.

● Younger children inevitably look up to their older counterparts. If they see positive role models, this will filter through into an improved ethos for the school.

Tips, ideas and activities

● Timetable a period of whole school reflection and self-evaluation during the week, introducing a 'Reflection log'. Request that pupils right across the school spend a short time in private, individual thought about their feelings, achievements and experiences. Adapt the format for recording reflections to the age of the children. For example:

- Reception-age children might be given a sheet showing faces with different emotions. They could colour in three feelings they have experienced that week.
- Year 1 and 2 children could be given a sheet with blanks to fill in, for example, *This week I enjoyed my … lesson most, I did a good piece of work in….*
- Older children might do a mind map of their successes, or write a few sentences about what they have done well.
- Ask the children to come up with their own formats for recording their reflections; some may wish to use artwork, photographs or diagrams.

● Give the children responsibility for a display area, with each year group or mix-aged groups being responsible for a weekly display.

● Introduce different themes for each week to run across the school. Use assembly time to share examples of what pupils have done around the theme and create a display to celebrate each week's theme. You could have:

- A 'Please and thank you' week
- A 'Be nice to others' week
- A 'Good listening' week
- A 'My favourite book' week.

● Set up school councils so that children from different year groups can get involved in thinking about and contributing to the running of the school.

● Organise a whole-school recycling project. Ask each class to think about:

- Which resources are being wasted in the school
- How these things might be collected up
- How they can be recycled
- Whether this should happen on site (for example, putting shredded paper on a compost heap) or through a local council collection.

You Can... # Think about time passing

For young children, time is a tricky concept to grasp. It is reasonably easy for them to learn to read the time from a clock. However, the thinking processes that help us understand the notion of time passing are of a higher order altogether.

Thinking points

● Partitioning up and structuring time helps us to create routines. The smooth and effective running of our schools is very much based around time structures.

● Sometimes, excessive structure can mitigate against learning. There needs to be some flexibility with the timing of thinking-based tasks, for example, where an interesting discussion is underway.

● Children generally appreciate time structures and routines. They help them prepare mentally for what is coming next.

● Where timing or routine is thrown, for example, through the absence of a class teacher, children may feel unsettled and confused.

● An understanding of longer periods of time comes slowly. At first children are limited to the short term; in ten minutes, after lunch, next week. Gradually they start to widen their perspective to next month, next year, a century ago.

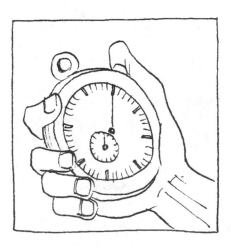

Tips, ideas and activities

● Use a display to show how we mark time passing in different ways. You could have:
  ● the names of the months
  ● the names of the seasons
  ● the year and a timeline
  ● the days of the week
  ● a weekly timetable
  ● a daily timetable
  ● different kinds of clock: digital clock, stopwatch, standard clock face, grandfather clock, candle and water clocks
  ● words relating to time, for example, yesterday, today, tomorrow, next week.

● Use your display during the year to help develop thinking.
  ● Stick up the children's pictures and birthdays under the names of the months, in the right sequence.
  ● Create collages to show what we find in each season.
  ● Rewrite the timetable for a day.
  ● Use the time words as a framework for speaking or writing in different tenses; 'Yesterday I went to…', 'Tomorrow I am going to…'.

● Talk about why we need to measure time.
  ● What would happen if all our clocks were taken away?
  ● How did people know what time it was before they had clocks?
  ● Why do we divide time up into seconds, minutes, hours?
  ● What would happen if we didn't have a school timetable?

● Try this fun prediction exercise. It calms down the class and encourages the pupils to concentrate. It also gives the teacher a minute or two of relative peace. Here's how it works:
  ● Explain that, when you say 'Go', you are going to time a minute.
  ● Ask the pupils to close their eyes.
  ● Tell the children to put up a hand when they think a minute has passed.
  ● Give a reward to the child who comes closest to the correct time.
  ● Afterwards, discuss why the children raised their hands at different times.
  ● Try again, this time for two minutes.

You Can... **Think about the seasons**

Thinking about the seasons will help your children understand the passing of longer periods of time. It also helps them find connections to, and patterns within, the natural world around them.

Thinking points

● In an urban environment, there will be less obvious signs of seasonal change. Exploring the seasons will encourage the children to look at and think about the natural aspects of the world around them.

● There are lots of scientific questions raised by the seasons. Thinking about what changes, and how it changes, will encourage your children's sense of curiosity.

● Work on the seasons can be linked to thinking about some of the festivals that take place during each season: Bonfire Night, Christmas, Easter, Divali. Eid and so on.

Tips, ideas and activities

● Use the photocopiable sheet 'Seasons: Odd one out' (see page 60) with your class. The pictures encourage information processing, with the children sorting and classifying the details in each picture to name the seasons. They will also be analysing the relationship between the picture and the season to identify the 'odd one out'.

● Use some seasons-related 'Why do you think…?' questions with your pupils. At this age, the children's answers may not be accurate, and the science behind the seasons may be too complex for them to understand. However, these questions will get them using a range of thinking skills: generating ideas, hypothesising, predicting, drawing conclusions, inferring and making deductions.
  ● Why do you think animals have their babies in the spring?
  ● Why do you think we get more daylight in the summer?
  ● Why do you think leaves fall from the trees in autumn?
  ● Why do you think it gets colder in the winter?

● Use tape to mark out a 'Seasons circle' on your classroom window. At various points during the year, get the children to look through the circle to gather information about what they can see. They might produce drawings, collages or take photographs to record the changing seasons.

● Plant some bulbs with your children in September or October:
  ● Choose bulbs that grow easily on top of the soil, such as daffodil, hyacinth or crocus. This keeps the changes visible, so the children can follow their progress.
  ● Get a fairly shallow pot or container; make sure that it has a hole in the base.
  ● Put some stones or gravel for drainage at the bottom, then fill the pot up with soil.
  ● Push the bulbs lightly into the soil with the growing points upwards.
  ● Water in, then keep slightly moist, but do not over-water.
  ● Try growing one bowl inside and one outside, to explore the difference that heat and light levels make to growth.

You Can... Explore the symbolism of festivals

You might celebrate a range of festivals with your children during the course of the school year. You can use the theme of festivals to develop thinking skills, by getting the children to look for patterns and associations between the different celebrations.

Thinking points

● Just as the seasons give a pattern to the course of each year, so the year is also punctuated by a series of festivals.

● These celebrations, whether religious or secular, have a great many symbolic gestures and traditions in common.

● Children can find many patterns and associations between the festivals. This can help promote a sense of inclusiveness, showing them how people from different cultures and faiths can be linked by common experiences.

● An understanding of the concept of symbolism, of one thing 'standing for' another, is an important thinking skill for the children to develop.

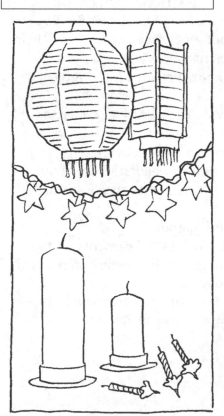

Tips, ideas and activities

● Together create a list of things that the children associate with a range of religious and secular festivals.
  ● Bonfire night: bonfires, fireworks, Guy Fawkes
  ● Divali: candles, lamps, fireworks, exchange of sweets, cards
  ● Christmas: trees, crackers, baubles, the Nativity, presents, cards, lights
  ● Chinese New Year: animals, dragons, decorations
  ● Easter: eggs, bunnies, hot cross buns, Jesus on the cross
  ● Carnival: parties, processions, dancing, costumes, music.

● Think about traditions that are linked with more than one festival. For example:
  ● giving and receiving presents
  ● decorations
  ● lights, such as candles and lanterns
  ● dancing, singing and music
  ● sending and receiving cards
  ● special foods.

● Show the class some gift-wrapped presents and ask:
  ● What do you think is inside?
  ● When in the year do you get presents?
  ● Does everyone get a present at these times?
  ● How does it feel to be given a present?
  ● How do you feel when you give someone else a present?
  ● What do you think it might mean when we give and receive presents?
  ● Does a gift have to be something we have bought?
  ● Can you think of any stories where someone gives or gets presents?

● Show the class a range of lights (candles, lanterns, fairy lights) and ask:
  ● When in the year do we use these kinds of lights?
  ● What seasons do these festivals fall in?
  ● Do you think there is a link between winter time and festivals that use lights?
  ● How do you feel when you see lights on a dark night?
  ● What is the difference between an electric light and a candle?
  ● Why do you think we blow out the candles on a birthday cake?

You Can... Use birthdays as a theme for thinking

Birthdays provide a useful theme for thinking, particularly about the passing of time. The special nature of birthdays will make each one a memorable occasion for your children.

Thinking points

● Aim to mark the birthday of each child in your class during the year. You might give cards, or simply ask the class to sing 'Happy birthday'.

● Check to see whether your school has a 'birth day' and when any particular milestones are being celebrated, such as fifty or even a hundred years. Some fascinating history work could arise from such a celebration.

● At Christmas time, it is worth reminding your children that this festival actually marks the birth of Jesus. The story of the Nativity can get rather forgotten in the whirl of presents, parties and food.

● You might also look at how the births of other religious figures are marked, for instance, Janmasthami is the Hindu celebration of the birth of Lord Krishna.

Tips, ideas and activities

● Create a spidergram for the word 'birthday'.
  ● As a whole class, write up ideas on the board.
  ● In small groups, draw pictures of things connected with birthdays.
  ● Use the word 'birthday' as a word association exercise in circle time.
  ● Use the word 'birthday' to create an acrostic poem.

● Talk with the class about the main features of a birthday, such as presents, cards, spending time with family, cakes, candles, parties, singing and dancing, party games and so on. Encourage them to think about why we do these things on a birthday.

● Ask the children if they can think of anyone whose birthday is celebrated by lots of people. They might talk about Jesus, Mohammed, other religious figures and perhaps the Queen.

● Get the class to plan a birthday party for a favourite character. Here are some suggestions for activities that you could do.
  ● Read the class some books featuring birthdays, such as *Kipper's Birthday* by Mick Inkpen (Hodder Children's Books) and *Spot's Birthday Party* by Eric Hill (Puffin Books).
  ● Talk with the children about what they like to do on their birthdays, and what these characters like to do.
  ● Help the class pick a well-known character for 'Project birthday party'.
  ● Think about and discuss what this particular character would like to do on his or her birthday.
  ● Plan and make a cake. Buy and weigh out the ingredients, decide how it will be decorated, work out how to divide it up amongst the guests and how much other party food to buy.
  ● Together make a list of party games.
  ● Use a catalogue to make a 'wish list' of presents for the character. What kind of things would they like to receive?
  ● Design and create a birthday card.
  ● Make a list of other favourite characters to invite to the party. Design, make and write some invitations.

You Can... Think about holidays

The holidays give your children (and you) a welcome opportunity to rest and recharge the batteries. Of course they can also be a wonderful learning experience, especially for those children who are lucky enough to travel.

Thinking points

- Children (and indeed teachers too) will often divide the school year up into 'How long is it until the next holiday?'

- It can be hard to keep your class focused and working hard as the holidays approach, particularly at Christmas time when there is so much else going on.

- Routines are often disrupted towards the end of terms, with extra assemblies, rehearsals for school shows and so on.

- The children might begin to push at the boundaries in terms of behaviour towards holiday time, particularly if you let them relax too soon. This can make the last few days of the term stressful, rather than restful, for the teacher.

- Let your children know in advance exactly when you are going to do some 'end of term' fun activities, whether this is the last week or the last day.

Tips, ideas and activities

- Have a general discussion about holidays, thinking from a range of perspectives.
  - What does the word 'holiday' mean?
  - What do we do during a holiday?
  - Why do we have holidays?
  - What makes a good holiday?
- Create a 'countdown' to the holidays. This is particularly helpful at Christmas, when the children might want you to relax the work ethic rather earlier than you see fit! You could:
  - Use or adapt an advent calendar.
  - Create a 'number of days left' calendar, counting down from ten to zero.
  - Add a 'thought for the day' related to learning on each page.
  - As a reward, choose a child to tear off each day's number and read out the quote.
- Use the theme of 'packing for a holiday' to inspire maths work on shape and space.
  - Show the class different sized suitcases and a pile of holiday packing.
  - Ask which case they think will fit the most packing.
  - Test out their theories.
  - Develop this with some group work fitting boxes inside each other.
- Have a class teddy that goes home with the children at weekends and during holidays. Use your travelling teddy to encourage thinking and learning across the curriculum.
  - Teddy keeps a diary of his adventures while he is away and the child reads this to the class.
  - Teddy has his photo taken next to interesting landmarks. The children try to identify where teddy is.
  - Teddy sends a postcard to the class.
  - Teddy brings back a souvenir for the class. The child talks about what teddy chose and why.
  - Mark the places teddy has gone on a large world map.
  - Explore the forms of transport that teddy used during his travels.
  - Examine the impact teddy's travels have on the environment. This is a good way of ensuring that those children who holiday in the UK can feel positive about taking teddy.

You Can... Build a 'community of enquiry'

As members of a 'community of enquiry', you and the children engage in philosophical discussions. Where discussion sessions are held regularly and are well managed by staff, the children can really learn to develop and extend their thinking.

Thinking points

● Philosophical discussions and other related activities, can help your children build a range of skills. These skills will feed into their learning across the curriculum.

● Taking part in these discussions will help your children develop their thinking skills. They learn to ask questions, to discuss and develop ideas, express and understand different opinions and so on.

● In addition to developing their thinking, the children will also be practising many important life skills. They will be learning to communicate effectively, to listen to each other, to share ideas, to respect other people's thinking and so on.

● For many children, these discussions can also lead to personal growth, for example, increased self esteem and confidence.

Tips, ideas and activities

● The term 'community of enquiry' is used to describe a group of children and their teacher involved in a philosophical discussion. Look at www.sapere.net and www.p4c.org.nz for more information and ideas.

● Before you begin your discussions, set some basic ground rules about attitudes and behaviour. You will need to revisit these rules as you go along, reinforcing any areas which the children find difficult. You might like to talk about the reasons for these ground rules as part of your philosophical discussions. The participants should:

  ● Remember that discussion is not about giving right or wrong answers.
  ● Be willing to participate and ask questions.
  ● Listen carefully to what other people say.
  ● Think carefully about what they are going to say.
  ● Aim to express their ideas in a clear way.
  ● Respect different opinions and points of view.
  ● Be open to new ideas and be willing to change their minds.
  ● Reflect on what they hear during the sessions.
  ● Aim to use a range of thinking skills; logic, creativity, reasoning, and so on.

● Be aware that your role is as a guide and facilitator in the discussion, rather than trying to force the children's thinking in any particular direction. It can feel a little uncomfortable at first taking on this role.

● The basic format of the sessions is:

  ● You begin by showing the class a stimulus to get the thinking going. This is often a story with a philosophical idea in it, but it might also be a picture, an object, a video, a poem, a letter and so on.
  ● You talk together to devise a series of possible questions for discussion arising from this stimulus.
  ● The class chooses one idea for extended discussion, with your help.
  ● Some potential topics might include: *What is right? What is wrong? What is good? Is it better to be good or to be happy?*

You Can... Think about friendship

For many children, spending time with their friends is one of the great benefits and joys of school. In the classroom, they will probably work well together with their friends. In the playground, they will enjoy letting off steam together.

Thinking points

● Most of the children in your class will find it relatively easy to make friends. These friends will help them feel comfortable and settled at school.

● Watch that you do not always let children work in friendship groups; this can lead to off-task behaviour as they chat socially. It can also mean that those who are not in a friendship group feel left out.

● There may be some children who struggle to make friends, and consequently feel lonely and isolated. The teacher should watch out for these pupils and try to help them settle in where possible.

● The behaviour of overly aggressive children might push their peers away. The same can apply to highly intelligent and able children whose academic abilities are more developed than their social skills.

Tips, ideas and activities

● Pick a book about friends as a stimulus for discussion. You might try:
   ● *Do You Want to Be My Friend?* by Eric Carle (Puffin Books)
   ● *My Friend Bear* by Jez Alborough (Walker Books)
   ● *Elmer's New Friend* by David McKee (Andersen Press).

● Use some proverbs, quotes and sayings to open up a discussion about what friendship is.
   ● 'If you live in the river, you should make friends with the crocodile.' (Indian proverb)
   ● 'I destroy my enemy when I make him my friend.' (Abraham Lincoln)
   ● 'The only way to have a friend is to be one.' (Ralph Waldo Emerson)
   ● 'Friendship is a sheltering tree.' (Samuel Coleridge)

● Use questions about friendship as a starting point for a discussion.
   ● What is a friend?
   ● What makes a 'good' friend?
   ● What is a best friend?
   ● Can a boy and a girl be best friends?
   ● How do we make friends?
   ● Can you buy friendship with money or gifts?
   ● Which famous person would you like to be friends with and why?
   ● Which character in a story would you like to be your friend and why?
   ● How do you think it feels if you don't have any friends?

● Explain to the children that a fictional 'new pupil' is going to join their class. Your fictional new child might be invisible, an alien, or a toy. Ask the children to help the new child settle in by:
   ● Creating a set of instructions on 'How to make friends'
   ● Drawing a picture of themselves and labelling it with tips on 'Being a good friend', for example, smile, listen, share
   ● Telling the class three reasons why 'I would make a good friend for you'.

● Talk with the class about why some children might find it hard to make friends:
   ● being new to an area or school
   ● being shy or quiet
   ● being an only child
   ● the other children in the class already having friendship groups.

You Can... Develop an understanding of respect

Disrespectful attitudes between children can be the cause of much tension. Where respectful relationships can be developed, this leads to a good atmosphere for learning and to far better behaviour.

Thinking points

- Children and young people are ever more aware of the term 'respect', but some of them seem to lack an understanding of what the concept actually means.

- A key skill in being respectful to others is being able to empathise; to see how our behaviour might make others feel.

- Encourage empathy by giving your pupils occasional insights into your emotional state. Let them know if you are unwell, or talk to them about how you feel when they disrupt a lesson that took you ages to plan. Do it sparingly; strike a balance between giving them glimpses of you as a person and having a good moan!

Tips, ideas and activities

- Talk with the class about what the word 'respect' means.
  - Being kind; treating others as you want to be treated.
  - Being polite; not calling other people names.
  - Listening to what other people have to say.
  - Treating everyone equally.
- Encourage your children to think about how and when we might show respect beyond our treatment of other people.
  - Looking after classroom equipment.
  - Taking care of the environment in and beyond the school.
  - Being kind to animals.
  - Treating the natural world with respect.
- Set some questions for discussion, based around the concept of respect.
  - Is it alright to be rude about people behind their backs, so long as they do not hear what you have said?
  - What kind of insults do the children hear at school? Have they insulted someone or been insulted themselves?
  - Why do some people get picked on and how do they think it makes them feel?
- Explore how we sometimes make immediate judgements about people and why these judgements might be prejudiced and disrespectful. Show the children pictures of a range of people and ask them to give their reactions to:
  - a person wearing torn and dirty clothes
  - a person with a shaven head or other unusual haircut
  - a very fat or thin person.

You Can... Explore different cultures and faiths

We live in an increasingly diverse society, in which many different peoples live and work alongside each other. As teachers we play a key part in encouraging children to explore a variety of cultures and faiths.

Thinking points

● Where prejudice exists, this is often caused by a lack of understanding and a limited range of experience. The classroom provides an ideal place for children to learn about and understand people from different cultural backgrounds.

● In urban settings, where there is often wide diversity, children will typically have experience of a range of cultures. However, there might also be tensions between different communities in your area.

● Where a class or school does not have a wide cultural mix, it is perhaps even more important to help the children learn about other races and religions.

● Teachers are not immune to cultural bias and we need to be aware of our own subconscious assumptions about children from different backgrounds. For example, remembering that direct eye contact is viewed as disrespectful in some cultures.

Tips, ideas and activities

● Talk about what the words 'racism' and 'prejudice' mean. Ask the children to think about why it is wrong to treat people differently according to their skin colour, religion and so on.

● Ensure that your classroom reflects a range of cultures and faiths. Check that resources, displays, texts and other materials take account of ethnic and religious diversity. Look also to challenge other stereotypes, such as traditional gender roles and ideas about people with disabilities.

● Celebrate different cultures by using activities that involve a wide range of cultural input.

  ● Ask the children to bring in something from their culture, for example, a book, a food or a toy.
  ● Bring in or cook foods from other countries.
  ● Explore decorations and patterns from other countries, for example, origami or Islamic mosaics.

● Hold 'cultural weeks', where the class or school explores a different culture. Involve parents in the planning and organisation. Activities and events can take place in lessons, but also at playtime (games from other countries), at lunchtimes (different ethnic foods) and after school (language clubs).

● Ask the children to research their family histories, to see whether they have some ancestors who originated in other countries.

● Create a calendar of religious festivals and celebrations for your classroom. See www.bbc.co.uk/religion/interactive/calendar/index.shtml for details and dates.

● Look at words and languages from other cultures.

  ● Ask volunteers to teach the class words in another language. This can really boost the self confidence of second language learners.
  ● Display samples of other languages around the room, including a range of scripts and alphabets.
  ● Get your children to research the origins of their names. They might ask their parents where their names came from or look online at www.behindthename.com
  ● Examine some words that came originally from other countries, and ask the children to try and guess their origins, for example. khaki, siesta, veranda, hamburger, ketchup, igloo and wigwam.

You Can... Think about viewpoints and opinions

For the very youngest children, the world often revolves around their own needs, wants and feelings. They find it hard to understand that other people might think differently to themselves and they only gradually learn to appreciate other points of view.

Thinking points

● Children need to hear a range of views and opinions so that they can gather the information required to make up their own minds. Teachers can offer them perspectives that might vary from what they hear in the home.

● Some subjects raise very strong opinions and viewpoints and you need to be sensitive to the children's emotional responses.

● Understanding that people think and feel differently plays a key role in the development of empathy.

● Even the youngest children can feel some sense of empathy; feeling sorry for mum if she is upset and trying to make her feel better.

Tips, ideas and activities

● Use fictional scenarios to help the children think about why different people might feel differently about the same situation.
  ● James hates PE but Tommy loves PE. The teacher says that PE is cancelled. How does James feel? How does Tommy feel?
  ● Amy is good at English and enjoys tests; Joanna has poor spelling and gets nervous. The teacher sets a spelling test. How does Amy feel? How does Joanna feel?
● Use fairy stories to look at different character perspectives. For example:
  ● 'Cinderella'; talk about the story from the point of view of the Ugly Sisters
  ● 'Little Red Riding Hood'; think about events from the wolf's point of view
  ● 'The Princess and the Pea'; consider what happens from the perspective of the pea.
● Develop this by using an exercise called the 'Judgement chair'. This will help your children think about different perspectives.
  ● Place a chair at the front. This is the 'Judgement chair'.
  ● Put a character from one of the stories into the chair. Play this character yourself or choose a volunteer.
  ● Children approach the chair as other characters in the story.
  ● They pass judgement on the character, saying what they think of that person's behaviour.
  ● The character being judged can listen silently or reply.
  ● For example, the wolf from 'Little Red Riding Hood'; the grandmother says, 'How dare you lock an old lady in the wardrobe like that!' and the wolf answers, 'I was hungry and you got in the way!'
● For a fun way to think about different points of view:
  ● Bring in a selection of footwear: trainers, men's shoes, wellington boots, high heels, sandals, slippers.
  ● Pick volunteers to come to the front and wear the shoes, literally 'standing in someone else's shoes'.
  ● Talk about the kind of person who wears these shoes.
  ● Discuss what these people might think about a range of issues.

You Can... # Develop strategies for reading and spelling

Teaching children to read is a subject that provokes seemingly endless controversy. Like much else in learning, the wider the range of strategies you teach your pupils, the better equipped they will be to use what works best for them.

Thinking points

● Because we learn to read so young, very few of us have strong memories of how we actually acquired this skill.

● Various thinking skills come into play in reading and spelling. The more strategies your children apply, the better able they will be to decode or write known and unfamiliar words.

● We can use prediction and deduction to work out words, by applying our prior knowledge of how letters and letter blends sound.

● We can use the context in which we find a word to hypothesise about what it might say. Pictures or storylines help us to work out a word that we don't yet recognise.

● Once we have seen words a number of times, we also use memory to recognise them by sight. This allows us to stop 'sounding out' individual words and consequently to become much faster readers.

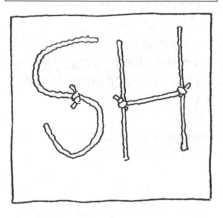

Tips, ideas and activities

● Use the senses and a range of learning styles, to help your children learn and retain new letters, letter blends and words. Lots of repetition in different formats will help the strategies 'stick', particularly for children who struggle with literacy.

● Find lots of different speaking and listening approaches, chants, rhymes, songs and so on to get the class hearing and using different sounds. Ask the children to think about how the look of some letters can be connected to their sounds:
  ● The letter S is the same shape as a snake and makes an 'sss' sound, like a snake
  ● The letter O is a round shape like a mouth forming a circle, which is how we make the 'O' sound.

● Use the alphabet to generate strings of rhyming words, from A to Z.
  ● Choose a letter blend, such as 'at'.
  ● Go through the alphabet, stopping every time the children spot a word.
  ● Write the word or draw a picture of it.
  ● In this instance: *bat, cat, fat, hat, mat, pat, rat, sat, vat.*

● Kinaesthetic approaches are a good way of making learning fun and memorable. The more active your learners are, the more likely they are to remember.
  ● Create letter sculptures, using modelling materials.
  ● Paint letter shapes in different sizes and colours.
  ● Create letters with different textures, related to their sounds; a shiny S or a rough R.
  ● Make the shapes of letters with your fingers or write big letters in the air.
  ● Make letter shapes with your bodies, individually or in groups.
  ● Create letter shapes out of pipe-cleaners.
  ● Do some super-sized letter sculptures out of boxes, kitchen rolls and so on.

● Use visual prompts (flash cards, displays, labels) to help your children recognise high frequency words. Make some memorable pictures that use the shape of the word to help show its meaning, for example putting eyes on the word 'see'.

You Can... **Explore effective characters**

Children often associate very strongly with the characters that they meet in stories. These associations can assist their social and emotional development, helping them learn how to empathise, how to deal with difficult emotions or events and so on.

Thinking points

● Even those children who are not familiar with many book-based characters will probably have 'met' a range of different characters on the television and in videos, DVDs, films.

● Some children do not get much access to literature outside of school. Showing them the links between books and other forms of media (television, comics, magazines and so on) will help engage them with reading.

● Children can use story characters to help them understand their own emotions. For example, a nervous child might associate strongly with a nervous character in a story. Seeing how this character copes can help the child gain in confidence.

● Some modern children's books have characters who challenge stereotypical thinking. These characters can encourage the children to develop more inclusive and positive attitudes to gender and race.

Tips, ideas and activities

● Explain to the children that you have been approached by a TV company which is developing a new children's television programme. They want the class to come up with suggestions for a new character.

● Together, create a list of the different characters the children can think of from books, television, film, comics and so on. Create a scattergram or an A to Z of characters. Consider their attributes:
  ● What do they look like?
  ● How do they behave?
  ● What are they called and why have these names been chosen?
  ● What happens to them in the stories?
  ● What sort of personalities do they have?
  ● What relationships do they have?
  ● Why are they appealing?
  ● Are there any you don't like and why?
  ● What age groups are they for and why?
  ● Are they aimed at boys/girls and why do you think this?

● Ask: *What makes a good character?* Talk through the characters from your list; which ones are powerful, interesting and engaging and why?

● Ask the children to bring in an example of a 'good' character. This might be from a book, a comic, a video, a toy from a television programme and so on. In groups, ask the children to talk about their chosen characters, saying why they picked this particular one.

● Ask the children to gather and develop ideas, devising a new character of their own, individually or in groups. Encourage a range of approaches to the thinking process.
  ● Use modelling materials to try out different ideas.
  ● Make collages using pictures torn from magazines.
  ● Research ideas by using reference materials.
  ● Interview other children to gather opinions.

● Ask the children to present their finished ideas to the class. You might invite 'representatives' of the television company in to hear the presentations (perhaps some parents or support staff).

● Ask the children to evaluate the ideas, encouraging them to consider what was most effective about their thinking and why.

You Can... **Think about storylines and sequencing**

All stories have a natural 'shape' or internal structure; at the most basic level a beginning and an end, but also a climax and a resolution. This shape aids our understanding and also adds to our enjoyment in reading a story.

Thinking points

● Your children will be using logical thinking to work out the 'correct' order of a storyline. They might also apply some creativity to bend and adapt the sequence of events in a variety of ways.

● Understanding structure and sequence will help your children create their own good quality stories, whether as spoken role plays or later on in extended writing.

● When you read stories to your class, you will be using your voice to suggest the internal structure, perhaps without even realising it. For example, you might quicken the pace or raise your tone as the story moves towards its climax.

Tips, ideas and activities

● Use the photocopiable sheet 'Storylines: Our trip to the beach' (see page 61) to teach your children about sequencing story events. The pictures are mixed up and the pupils must put them in order.

● Use the photocopiable sheet to stimulate thinking. With the youngest children you might:

○ Identify the beginning and end of the story. Talk with the children about how they worked this out

○ Get the children to colour in the pictures. Working as a whole class, help the pupils sequence the story

○ Ask the children whether they can think of a more interesting opening or ending for the story

○ In pairs, ask the pupils to re-tell the story to their partners

○ Talk with the class about which part of the story is most exciting for the child involved and for the reader.

● Make a baby book called 'At the beach' showing sand, shells, buckets and so on with labels.

● With older or more able pupils, you might:

○ Ask the children to cut out the pictures, sticking them on paper in sequence.

○ Talk about whether there is more than one possible order and which order is potentially most interesting.

○ Give the children cards with words used to structure time, such as *first, next, after, when, eventually* and *finally*.

○ Ask them to write a sentence for each picture using the appropriate time word.

○ Make a book called 'My trip to the beach'.

○ Write a postcard home or a diary of the trip.

○ Write some timelines or flow charts showing events from the course of a day, perhaps about a recent class trip.

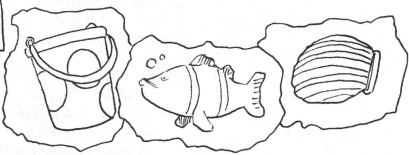

You Can... Think about how punctuation works

Accurate punctuation is one area of writing where many children struggle, even during their secondary school careers. They might understand how to use punctuation correctly, but find it difficult to translate this into their writing.

Thinking points

● We might try to 'hammer home' a particular type of punctuation (full stops, speech marks), by using repetitive exercises. Unfortunately, some children quickly slip back into making mistakes when they are doing free writing.

● Being able to punctuate correctly is not just about the technical knowledge of where a full stop or comma should go. It is even more important that children understand how punctuation influences the sound of writing.

● Encourage your children to hear their writing in their heads, before they put it down on page. This will help them focus on how it should sound, and hopefully translate this into correct punctuation.

● An overemphasis on correct grammar and accurate punctuation can stifle the early writer. Make sure that you also give your children time to write without worrying overly about technique.

Tips, ideas and activities

● Talk with your children about the logic behind punctuation, as well as how it actually works, making sure the learning 'sticks':
  ● Create vivid and memorable associations.
  ● Use strong vocal emphasis in explanations.
  ● Create 'big' images in the children's minds.
  ● Look for shapes, links and patterns.
  ● Use practical, physical activities.
  ● Actively involve the children in the learning.
  ● Use songs, rhymes and mnemonics.
  ● Take imaginative approaches, for instance a child playing a police officer who shouts 'Stop!' at the end of sentences.

● To give an example, when thinking and talking about the logic of capital letters, you might point out that:
  ● A capital is a 'big' letter.
  ● Words that get capitals are big, important words, such as our names.
  ● 'I' am very important; therefore 'I' get a capital.
  ● The start of a sentence is its highest point, falling down towards the full stop.

● Use this 'cut and paste' punctuation activity, to get your children punctuating different texts.
  ● Choose an appropriate piece of text for your class.
  ● Take a photocopy of the text and white out all the punctuation (copyright permitting).
  ● Create a 'bank' of the missing punctuation at the bottom of the page. In this 'bank', put the correct number of full stops, commas, speech marks and so on.
  ● Ask the children to read the text several times, thinking about punctuation. Do this at least once out loud, sounding out pauses, exclamations and so on.
  ● Get the children to add the punctuation back in, ensuring that they use up all the marks in their 'bank'.

● Sometimes, let your children write without concerns over technique.
  ● Do a 'stream of consciousness'; the children write whatever comes into their minds for a minute.
  ● Tape the children's ideas and listen back to them.
  ● Use a support teacher as a scribe.
  ● Write ideas straight onto a computer.

You Can... **Think about giving instructions**

There are a whole host of thinking skills involved when your children learn to give instructions. They must use logic to work out the correct or most appropriate order, and they must also think about suiting their explanation to the appropriate audience.

Thinking points

● Teachers often become extremely expert at giving instructions to their classes. This is a skill that comes with practice; at first, there may be many cries of 'I don't understand what I'm meant to do' from your pupils.

● When explaining an idea or an activity, if the teacher's instructions are not clear and simple to follow, the children will often go off-task.

● For some children, listening to and understanding verbal instructions will prove very tricky. It is always worth backing up your spoken explanations with some writing or a diagram.

● If you have ever tried to assemble a piece of flat pack furniture from badly written instructions, you will know how important (and indeed, difficult) it can be to get it right!

Tips, ideas and activities

● Talk and think generally with the class about instructions.

  ● Discuss different kinds of instructions: recipes, safety guidelines, instructions booklets and so on.

  ● Think about why teachers have to give instructions: to explain a lesson, to ensure safe behaviour, to uphold rules.

  ● Consider when and why it is very important to follow instructions.

  ● Show the children a range of instruction booklets and leaflets.

  ● Identify the common features in different sets of instructions.

● Discuss the important elements of a set of instructions. For example, that they must be in the right order, clearly written, and easy to follow. Talk about the type of language used when giving instructions: direct, impersonal, imperative verbs.

● Talk about different ways of showing the correct order in instructions. For example: write a list, use numbered points, or use language that shows order (*first, next, then* and so on).

● Use an interesting focus to make the learning more engaging. For example, the children might give spoken or written instructions:

  ● to an alien who is new to the planet Earth

  ● to a character in a favourite book

  ● to someone who cannot see

  ● to someone who cannot read

  ● using only pictures.

● Give the class a list of useful verbs with which to write instructions. Include simple imperatives such as *put, take, turn, fold* and *pull*.

● Tell the children that you are an alien. Ask them to instruct you in a simple task (making a sandwich, washing your hands), taking everything they say completely literally.

● Write out a set of mixed-up instructions, such as a recipe. Ask the children to cut and paste these into the right order.

● Arrange the children into pairs, sitting back to back. Give one child a simple picture and the other some paper and a pencil. The children with the pictures must instruct their partners in how to draw the picture without seeing it. Repeat the exercise with one child explaining an unseen picture to the whole class.

You Can... **Think about shapes**

Shapes are all around us; once you start to look you can see them everywhere. Encouraging your children to look more closely develops their observational skills. It also helps them to see the links between maths and the real world.

Thinking points

● Shapes provide some fascinating material for thinking. They play an important role, not just in maths, but right across the curriculum. From art to religion, dance to science, shapes often come with many additional layers of meaning.

● It is of course important to teach children to be able to name different shapes. But we can go one step beyond this and get them thinking about how the shapes in maths relate to the world all around them.

● Playing with and manipulating shapes will help your children develop their mathematical thinking. The discoveries that they make will help engage them with the subject and lead them on to more complex maths skills in later years.

Tips, ideas and activities

● When studying shapes in maths, have a 'Shape of the week', using some or all of the activities below in connection with each shape. Alternatively, you might ask one group of children to do activities for circles, another for squares, another for triangles and so on.

● Go on a 'Shape hunt', looking for examples of the week's shape. You could set this up as a challenge between groups, with pupils listing, drawing or photographing all the different examples of the shape that they find.

● Encourage your children to think about the meanings and symbolism behind shapes. For example, when studying circles you could talk about:
  ● The circle having no beginning or end
  ● The symbolic use of circles for rings
  ● Circles used within different religions
  ● The equality of people when standing in a circle.

● Look through the alphabet with your class, to see how many shapes and parts of a shape, such as a circle, you can find in the different letters.

● Explore ways of making a shape with our bodies, different materials, and so on. For example, with circles:
  ● The class standing hold hands in a circle
  ● Making circles with their fingers
  ● Using string to make circles
  ● Using the base of a bottle to print circle shapes.

● Experiment with shapes to see what happens when they are chopped up in different ways. Use three-dimensional shapes, such as an orange or a clay ball, to explore what happens when these are divided.

● Ask the children to think about how they might use a shape for lots of different purposes. For example, they could use a circle for:
  ● playing games
  ● making sets in a maths lesson
  ● circle time
  ● making a wheel.

You Can... **Explore measurements**

One of the ways in which we impose a structure on our world is to create and use different forms of measurement. Our every day lives rely heavily on standard measures; from time to money, from cookery to transport.

Thinking points

● You can find examples of measurement everywhere around you at school; the standard school day is closely regulated by measuring time.

● Standardised measurements have evolved and changed over the years. You might like to talk and think with your children about why this is so.

● Children can find comparative measures quite a difficult concept to grasp, for example, understanding that one metre is equal to one hundred centimetres.

● When exploring these measures, it is useful and interesting to think about the roots of words, even with very young children. This can provide a useful memory 'hook' to help the pupils understand and retain the information. For example, the addition of 'cent' to create 'centimetre' (from the Latin 'Centurion', a soldier who commanded 100 men).

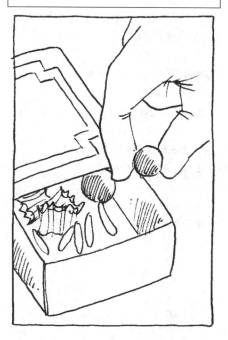

Tips, ideas and activities

● Create some interesting and useful 'thinking displays' around the subject of measuring.

  ● Together, write a list of vocabulary for estimating and create your own 'Rough guide to measuring'. Include words and phrases such as: *guess, roughly, about, approximately, around, more or less, nearly, give or take.*

  ● Make a list of comparative words and find interesting ways of illustrating these. For example, *long, longer* and *longest* might be shown by a giraffe in baby, child and adult size.

  ● Develop a display that shows all the different ways we use to measure our world. As you cover each area, add relevant vocabulary labels to the display. For example, the 'Measuring time' section would include *second, minute, hour* and so on.

● Come up with some interesting and imaginative formats for working with and writing about measurements.

  ● Use the *Meg and Mog* books by Jan Pienkowski (Ladybird Books) as an inspiration for creating some magic spell recipes.

  ● Devise a book or cartoon strip called 'Mr Measure', in the style of the *Mr Men* series (Egmont Books).

  ● Ask the children to write a recipe in time measurements for their ideal week; ten minutes at school, two hours at the park, thirty minutes eating chocolate, a whole day watching television!

● Think laterally when finding things to measure; the more original, unusual or humorous the better. Get the children to make estimates and predictions first and then check results by using a standardised measure or by counting.

  ● Measure round some unusual round fruits and vegetables, for example, pumpkins, melons, grapes, peas and so on.

  ● Measure round the heads of different members of staff (make sure you get their permission first!)

  ● Investigate how many small items they can fit in a matchbox; peas, pencil shavings, grains of rice and so on.

● Look at pictures of giant-sized things: large animals, big buildings, monster trucks or machines. Create some life-sized collages of large baby animals: a baby whale, a baby elephant or a baby hippo.

You Can... Use stories to practise problem solving

Daily life is full of problems that need solving and many of these problems involve some form of mathematical thinking. Showing your children how closely maths relates to their lives outside of school will help increase their motivation.

Thinking points

● Problem solving is much more interesting when it is given a wider context. Solving a series of problems in a story is a far more engaging activity than looking at individual problems in isolation.

● Looking at 'real life' problems will show your children how useful and vital maths is in dealing with their day-to-day lives.

● You can make the maths even more 'real' by using props and recreating or staging some problems to explore with the class.

Tips, ideas and activities

● Create a storyline around which your children solve a series of mathematical problems. Choose a fiction that will engage your pupils, for example:
  ● A trip to the shops
  ● A day out at the beach
  ● Stranded on a desert island.
● Depending on the age and ability levels of your children, you might explore these stories:
  ● As a whole class, solving each problem together through discussion and writing ideas on the board
  ● In small groups, with each group working on a different section of the story and reporting their results back to the class
  ● In pairs or individually, from a worksheet.
● A story called 'Match of the day' would work well for engaging football-mad boys or girls.
  ● Josh has to catch the bus to the football ground at 9am. He needs one hour to get dressed and have breakfast and quarter of an hour to walk to the bus stop. What time should he set his alarm?
  ● Josh has £5 to spend at the match. The bus costs 50p and the ticket for the match costs £2.50. How much money does he have left over?
  ● Josh's team wins by one goal. The total number of goals scored is five. How many goals does the other team score?
● Once your children have completed the problems, develop the work further by creating a display to retell the story.
  ● Split the class into groups and ask each group to work on a display for one section of the story.
  ● Get the children to set up their part of the story as a frozen picture and then take a digital photo.
  ● Write a caption for the photo explaining what the problem was and how it was solved.
  ● Ask the class to sequence the events in the right order.

You Can... **Think about money**

Even at a very young age, your children will already be aware of money; what it is and how it can be used. You can find some interesting and 'real life' ways to introduce them to the skills involved in working with money.

Thinking points

● The idea that pieces of metal and paper are 'worth' more than their literal value is an interesting concept to explore with your children.

● You will want to teach your children mathematical skills such as being able to pay the correct money and give change. You can also develop their thinking skills by looking at concepts such as value, worth and the fair distribution of wealth.

● Studying money gives plenty of opportunities for using props and fictional scenarios to help you engage your class with the learning.

Tips, ideas and activities

● Do some general thinking and talking about money.
  ● Show the class money from different countries and different historical periods. Compare these with modern day UK coins and notes.
  ● List the different ways we can pay for something: cash, cheques, credit cards, IOUs, and so on.
  ● Talk about how some people have lots of money and others have less.
  ● Discuss ways that we can get money: earn it, be given it for presents and pocket money and so on.
  ● Talk about how early people might have made payments, such as trading and bartering, primitive forms of money.
  ● Show the children a £5 note and a piece of paper with £5 written on it. Ask them which is worth more and why.
  ● Talk about cash as a symbol for representing payment and wealth.

● Put a range of coins in a 'feely bag'. Invite volunteers to come up and feel a coin and to try and guess what it is.

● For a fun mental arithmetic starter activity, try this 'hidden coins' exercise.
  ● Show the children a coin denomination (such as 1p, 2p or 5p).
  ● Take a tin or moneybox and ask the children to close their eyes.
  ● Drop several coins of the same denomination into the tin (for example, 5 x 1p).
  ● Pause after you drop each one so that the children can keep count in their heads.
  ● Ask the children to say how much money is now in the tin.
  ● Get a volunteer to come up and empty the tin to check.

● Create 'real life' situations involving money in a role-play area. Add 'real' resources, including tills, plastic or laminated cardboard coins, receipts, food and other items to 'buy'. Your settings might include:
  ● a supermarket
  ● a post office
  ● a café
  ● a fast food restaurant
  ● a fruit and vegetable shop
  ● a train station
  ● a newsagents
  ● a post office.

You Can... Create a mathematical mystery

Mysteries and puzzles are great for engaging your children's curiosity. Where the teacher makes the mystery come to life by creating a fictional scenario, this really hooks the children into the story, and into the thinking involved in finding a solution.

Thinking points

● Children are typically very knowledgeable about the vocabulary, imagery and ideas around detectives and crime scenes. They will often have seen television programmes, books or cartoons that use the genre of mystery.

● Keep the mysteries you create quite light-hearted, in case there are any sensitive souls in your class; no gruesome murders, no matter how tempting!

● Solving the mystery involves some mathematical thinking and reasoning skills. It also requires creative and imaginative thinking and the use of logic, deduction and hypothesising.

Tips, ideas and activities

● Create a 'crime scene' in your classroom. When the children arrive at the lesson, explain that they are going to be detectives. They have to solve the crime by using mathematical and other thinking skills.

● To add reality, use real life props as far as possible. For even greater authenticity, buy some police crime-scene tape online at www.uktapes.com.

● There are various ways to approach the activity, depending on the age of your children and the type of class. You might work as a whole class to think about and solve the mystery. You could start with an initial whole-class discussion and then split the children into groups to work on the scenario.

● Here is a description of a sample 'crime scene'. Explain to the children that, during break, someone broke into the classroom and took money from your purse. At this point make it clear to any sensitive children that this is a story and not real. At the crime scene have:

  ● one of the classroom windows slightly ajar
  ● a purse on a table with small change scattered around it
  ● a set of large footprints leading from the window to the purse and back.

● Discuss with the children about what they think has happened. Talk about the mathematical skills that your children might use to help them solve the crime, for example:

  ● Measure how far the window has been pushed open, to estimate the size of the 'burglar'
  ● Count and measure the footprints, to deduce the shoe size and height of the burglar
  ● Work out how much money has been taken
  ● Consider timing, for example, how long the crime would have taken to commit.

● For follow-up activities, you could:

  ● Ask the children to create a dramatised reconstruction of the crime
  ● Photograph the scene and add labels to describe each piece of evidence
  ● Create a storyline sequence to show what the children think has happened
  ● Write a police report about the crime
  ● Interview some suspects.

You Can... **Think about 'Toys'**

Not only is playing with toys great fun for children, they also learn a great deal from their play. Teachers can utilise the opportunities for learning around this topic, creating a project that really engages and involves the whole class.

Thinking points

● This project widens and builds on the theme 'toys'.

● There are so many imaginative and cross-curricular opportunities with this theme, that you may find it hard to work out what not to include!

● Children do often form very strong bonds and attachments to their toys and this creates a natural sense of interest and enthusiasm.

● This theme is useful for developing historical skills, such as language connected to the passing of time and also sequencing items into date order.

● It also offers many chances for imaginative, creative and unusual activities.

Tips, ideas and activities

● Create puzzles and mysteries using toys, to harness your children's curiosity.
  - Place toys in odd places around the room; suspend a teddy from the ceiling or put a doll on your chair.
  - Set up a toy treasure hunt with clues to solve.
  - Hide small toys in your sand-play area.
  - 'Kidnap' a toy, leaving a ransom note and asking the pupils to solve the crime.

● Use the run-up to Christmas to stimulate thinking around this theme.
  - Encourage your pupils to think about those children who might not get presents.
  - Create a 'Toy factory', asking Santa's elves to build new toys using packaging materials.
  - Plan and create a 'Santa's grotto'.

● Explore the issue of toy safety.
  - Examine a range of toys: *What age are they appropriate for and why?*
  - Design a toy that is suitable for a baby.

● Look at toys from other periods in history and cultures.
  - Ask the children to sequence old and new toys according to their age.
  - Highlight the vocabulary used when something is old (dusty, rusty, broken) or new (clean, fresh, modern).
  - Look at toys from other cultures, such as Russian dolls.
  - Think about primitive toys. Ask the children to make a toy or game out of naturally occurring materials, such as sticks, twine, stones and so on.

● Use toys to stimulate thinking about gender stereotypes.
  - Show the class a range of toys; bricks, dolls, teddies, dolls' houses, garages, games and so on.
  - Ask the children to sort these toys into those for boys, girls or either.
  - Talk about the thinking behind the choices they made.
  - Consider how toy manufacturers make toys appeal to one gender, for example, colour, advertising, vocabulary and so on.
  - Have a 'Toy swap' day, encouraging the children to play with toys associated with the opposite sex.

You Can... **Think about 'Ourselves'**

Young children have a great interest in themselves as a topic; at this age, they believe the world revolves around them and their needs. It is very useful for the teacher to find out how the children feel about themselves and what they do and do not enjoy.

Thinking points

● This is a great theme for helping you get to know your children better and it is a good one to cover right at the start of the school year.

● The topic offers plenty of opportunities for bringing in interesting and engaging resources. Parents who are doctors, dentists or nurses may be able to help you access information and materials.

● The ideas below build on the theme 'Ourselves', giving some ways of extending the work across the curriculum.

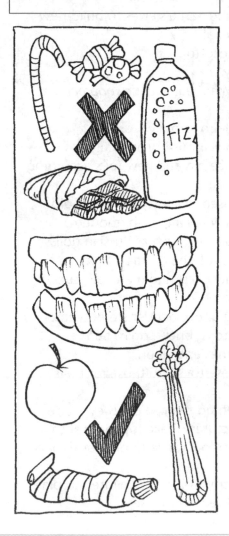

Tips, ideas and activities

● Think about ways of representing children in pictures and in artworks.

  ● Study some self-portraits by famous artists, for example those by Van Gogh, Rembrandt and Picasso. Talk about these pictures: *How did these artists feel about themselves when they were created?* Using mirrors, ask the children to create their own self-portraits in a variety of artistic techniques.

  ● Take digital photographs of the children, lying down on the floor, with tongues poking out. Add labels to these photos to show the different parts of the body.

  ● Create 'Mini me's': accurate, scaled-down pictures of themselves to go on the classroom wall.

● Explore your children's likes and dislikes. Take a picture of each child doing his or her favourite thing at school. Get the pupils to make a caption for the pictures and create a display.

● Look at body coverings; both on humans and animals. Create some textured collages to show fur, scales, feathers and so on.

● Introduce some work based on skeletons and body parts.

  ● Use the book *Funnybones* by Janet and Allan Ahlberg (Puffin Books) as a starting point for talking about skeletons.

  ● Build a human skeleton online; see www.bbc.co.uk/ schools/podsmission/bones/annie02.shtml.

  ● Get hold of some old X-rays to show your children. Check at your local hospital, or ask any parents who are doctors or dentists.

● Think about how we can keep our teeth healthy.

  ● Invite a dentist or dental technician to talk to the children about keeping their teeth healthy.

  ● Look at a range of things that we use in connection with our teeth and talk about how they are used and why.

  ● Create an 'Opposites' display to show things that are good or bad for your teeth. If possible, include some false teeth to make your display more eye-catching!

You Can... **Think about 'The moving world'**

Young children love to move and using movement as a topic for cross-curricular work gives you a great opportunity to capitalise on this fact. Choose a time when you are full of energy yourself for this busy and active theme.

Thinking points

● This project builds on and develops the theme of 'Pushes and pulls'.

● This is a great theme for your kinaesthetic learners. The lessons use practical, energetic activities to get the children thinking about how and why things move.

● There is a wide range of cross-curricular learning possible here, including some in PE, science, geography, maths and art.

● Many thinking skills will be used during this project, including predicting, hypothesising, drawing conclusions and so on.

● To extend the project even further, create a 'movement wall' in your classroom, to gather together examples of vocabulary, experiments, photographs, surveys and so on.

Tips, ideas and activities

● In a PE session encourage your children to think about how we move, and the vocabulary of movement. Create laminated movement cards, including words such as *twist*, *turn*, *spin* and *jump*. Ask the children to pick several cards at random and create a sequence from those movements.

● Perform experiments involving pushes, pulls and movements in the playground. Work as a whole class, using volunteers to demonstrate, or create a 'round robin' with groups rotating every ten minutes.

  ● Explore moving toys: bicycles, scooters, skateboards and so on. *What makes them move? Can we move them without pushing?* (Stand sideways on the skateboard and swing your arms side to side.)

  ● Push and blow different toy boats across a tank of water. *Which boat moves furthest and why?*

  ● Blow up balloons to different sizes; predict which will go furthest and why, then let them go.

  ● Blow water out through straws. *How can we make the water travel furthest?*

  ● Blow bubbles to see what happens when the wind catches them.

  ● Throw paper aeroplanes to see which shape goes furthest.

● Survey transport in the local area (cars, buses, people) and also look at weather movements (rain falling, wind blowing trees and clouds).

● Go to your local park to explore how children's playground equipment moves: swings, slides, roundabouts and so on. Send some balls down the slides; explore which goes furthest and why.

● Find rhymes and stories that include movement. For example: 'The Three Little Pigs' to experiment with different building materials, thinking about why the straw and brick houses can be blown over; 'Incy Wincy Spider' to show how water can move things.

● Explore artwork that involves movement, for example:

  ● Blow, flick or pull string through paint.

  ● Put a huge piece of paper outside and get the class to flick paint onto it.

  ● Look at the work of Jackson Pollock, an American artist whose techniques included dripping and throwing paint onto canvas.

You Can... **Think about 'Alien visitors'**

As a topic, the idea of aliens visiting from another planet will be very captivating for young children. Thinking about how these aliens might gather facts about our world offers an interesting way into the fairly dry topic of information.

Thinking points

● This topic provides a great way of exploring different perspectives; it asks how our world would appear to alien visitors who have never been here before.

● The type of material covered links and builds on the ICT theme 'The information around us'.

● There are lots of opportunities for imaginative and creative thinking around this topic.

● As well as considering how we find and access information, the pupils will also be sorting information into different types, and exploring how information can be communicated to others.

Tips, ideas and activities

● With your class, read some of the *Dr Xargle* books by Jeanne Willis and Tony Ross (Andersen Press). These books look at Earth from the perspective of visiting aliens.

● Ask the children to think about what life might be like on an alien planet.
  ● Look at information about our solar system.
  ● Make collages or three-dimensional models of their own alien planets.
  ● Create designs or models of strange modes of alien transport.
  ● Devise, illustrate and cook some recipes for alien foods.
  ● Draw and label pictures of some alien pets.

● Look at the photocopiable sheet 'Alien visitors' (see page 62) with your class. Talk about:
  ● What each picture is 'saying'.
  ● How this information is communicated; by sounds, by pictures, by text and so on.
  ● What 'type' of information it is, for example, a warning, a fact or an emotion.

● Colour in the pictures, then cut them out and sort in various ways. For example, according to:
  ● How they communicate; by using a noise, an image or print.
  ● What they communicate; a warning, a fact and so on.
  ● Where they are found; in a book, in a house, in a school or outside.

● Consider how to explain each thing to an alien visitor who knows nothing about life on Earth.
  ● The whistle; 'A teacher blows on a metal object, making a loud noise to say playtime is over.'
  ● The traffic lights; 'Three lights on the end of a big stick, red says stop, green says go.'

● Use media and ICT to look at different ways of communicating this information to alien visitors.
  ● Take digital photographs of 'real life' examples of each image and label them for a display.
  ● Download images or sounds from the internet, to show more examples of how we communicate information.
  ● Use a word processor to write and illustrate a new 'Dr Xargle' book.

You Can... **Think about 'Opposites'**

An important way of sorting and categorising our world is to think of it in terms of opposing pairs. Exploring different types of opposites will help your children think about how to match and sort and also to look for patterns in their thinking.

Thinking points

● As a theme, opposites can be used to cover every area of the curriculum; from English to art, from maths to RE

● You might link work on this theme into science topics, such as light and dark or pushes and pulls. You could connect it with work in PE or dance, on opposing movements.

● The concept of opposites and oppositions between forces has many philosophical implications. Notions of good and evil and of right and wrong are closely bound up with much religious and moral thinking.

Tips, ideas and activities
● Find as many opposites as you can:
  ● Light and dark
  ● Up and down
  ● Good and bad
  ● Full and empty
  ● Hot and cold.
● Think of symbols to represent each pair of opposites, for example, an arrow pointing for up and down. Work as a class, or ask volunteers to draw their ideas and get the children to guess the answer.
● In a PE, dance or drama lesson, encourage the children to create still images or mimed scenes to represent opposites. For example, one child walks very heavily, whilst the other bounces around as if in zero gravity.
● Use opposites as a theme for a music lesson, finding sounds that are loud and quiet, high and low, and so on.
● Create an opposites display, using colours, images and textures; rough and smooth, shiny and dull, black and white.
● Actively involve the children in creating examples of opposites, perhaps as a quick 'break out' exercise during longer periods of concentration.
  ● Being very noisy; then at a signal from you, becoming very quiet.
  ● Standing up very tall; then dropping down to be very small.
  ● Making very happy faces; then suddenly looking very sad.
● Play 'Opposites'.
  ● Give the children several blank pieces of card.
  ● On one card they should draw and label an opposite, then make the matching pair on another card.
  ● For example, they could draw a heavy weight with the word 'heavy' on one card, then a feather with the word 'light' on another.
    To play the game, lay the cards face down.
  ● The children take it in turns to turn two cards over.
  ● If the pair 'match' (are a pair of opposites), they keep the cards.
  ● If they do not match, the cards are turned back over and the game restarts.
  ● The aim is to collect the most cards by the end of the game.

Question and answer guidelines

We try to take part in question and answer sessions.

We put up our hands when we want to answer a question.

We wait to be asked before giving an answer.

We listen in silence when someone else is talking.

We let anyone and everyone give their ideas.

We show respect for what other people think and feel.

Thinking about behaviour

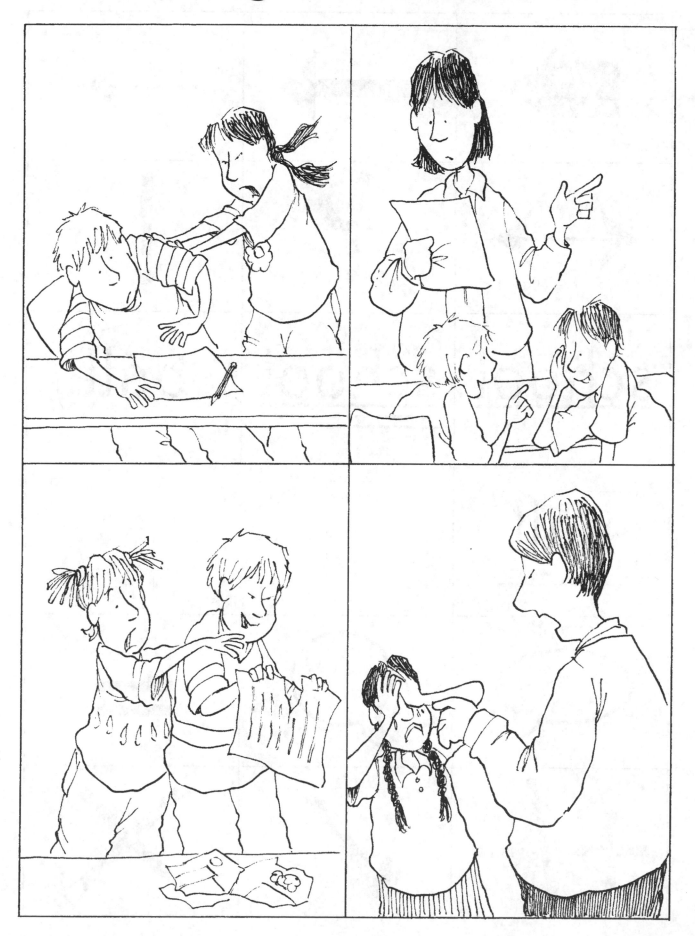

You Can... **Create a thinking classroom 4–7**

Symbols for thinking

➡	➡	→
↔	**?**	**!**
<u>school</u>	<u><u>school</u></u>	⬭ ball
ball	▭—▭	
💬	💬	**=**
+/-	✔	✗

The magic carpet

Seasons: Odd one out

Look at the four pictures.
- What season is it in each picture?
- Write the names of the seasons above the pictures.
- In each picture, there is something that does not belong. Draw a circle around the odd one out.
- Now colour in the pictures.

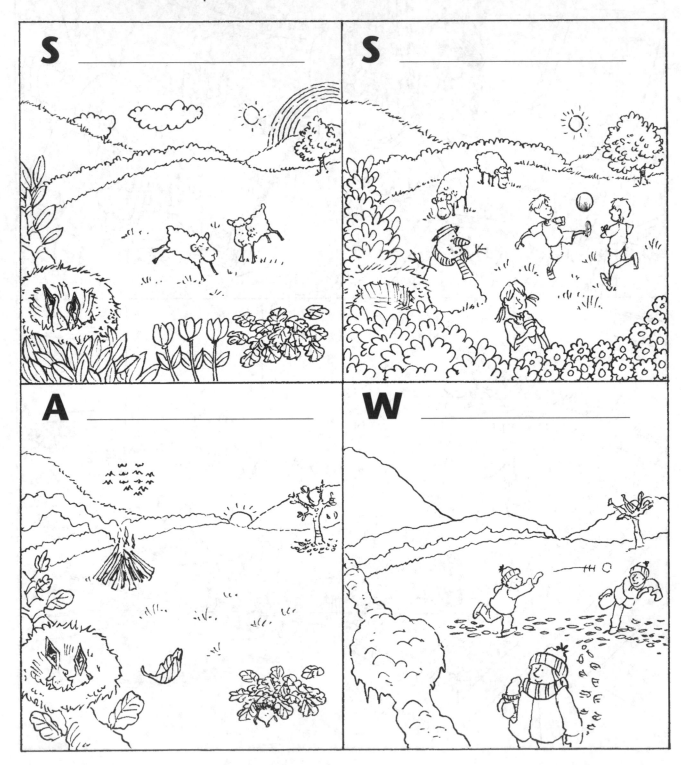

S _____

S _____

A _____

W _____

Storylines: Our trip to the beach

Alien visitors

Index

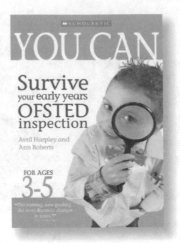